A BODY

ACROSS TWO

a memoir in essays

HEMISPHERES

VICTORIA BUITRON

PRAISE

A Body Across Two Hemispheres is a timely book, one many of us need and will be grateful to have read. There's much to praise about Victoria Buitron's debut. For starters, it showcases the author's formal range within the essay, collecting together lyric pieces, full-fledged narratives, and documentary collage—all of which interweave the personal story with political allegory. The book begins with the narrator's migration at fifteen, from the United States back to Ecuador, the country of her birth and one she left in early childhood. Centered in accounts of family and of multiple migrations, Buitron moves from adolescence into adulthood, laying claim to who she is by braiding together her various selves. Never shying from what is difficult to reconcile, *A Body Across Two Hemispheres* introduces an utterly engaging, assured new voice in nonfiction. In her memoir-in-essays, Buitron lays bare various forms of grief but presents them with equal measures of resilience. She posits love—ultimately—as the curative for loss.

—SHARA MCCALLUM, AUTHOR OF *NO RUINED STONE*
AND *THE FACE OF WATER*

A BODY ACROSS TWO HEMISPHERES

a memoir in essays

VICTORIA BUITRON

woodhall press
Woodhall Press
Norwalk, CT

woodhall press

Woodhall Press, 81 Old Saugatuck Road, Norwalk, CT 06855
WoodhallPress.com

Cover design: Danny Sancho
Layout artist: Amie McCracken

Library of Congress Cataloging-in-Publication Data available

ISBN: 978-1-949116-99-1
ISBN: 978-1-949116-62-5

First Edition

Distributed by Independent Publishers Group
(800) 888-4741

Printed in the United States of America

A Body Across Two Hemispheres is a work of nonfiction, but the writer
acknowledges that her truth may differ from the truth of others' lived
experiences. The names of certain individuals and locations in this book
have been altered to protect people's privacy.

For
Segundo Reinaldo Buitrón

The author is grateful to the editors of the publications in which the following essays have appeared:

"Cat Whistles and Wolf Calls" appeared in *Entropy.*

"Chain Migration" appeared in *Anomaly.*

"Changes" appeared in *Emerge Literary Journal.*

"Driving by Great Island on Chilly Evenings" appeared in *(mac)ro(mic)* and the title is a play on words inspired by Robert Frost's poem "Stopping by Woods on a Snowy Evening."

"First Comes the Egg" appeared in *Luna Luna Magazine.*

"Hair in Three Forms" appeared in *The Bare Life Review.*

"How to Be an Ecuadorian Girl" appeared in *The Nasiona.*

"Let It Burn" appeared in *Barren Magazine.*

"Teeth Fragments" appeared in *Bending Genres* and is written after "Bear Fragments" by Christine Byl.

"The First Test" appeared in *Jellyfish Review.*

"The Translator" appeared in *Citron Review.*

"(Un)Documented" is written after "The ABCs" by Adriana Páramo.

Home may be a mode of living made into a metaphor of survival.
—Homi K. Bhabha

CONTENTS

THE SOUTHERN HEMISPHERE

BODYBREAK

On the day of the cleanse, I learned that my shaman and I had similar first names. Before Victor arrived that evening, I wondered what he would look like. I imagined he lived in a hut made of straw and hid his penis with a loincloth that wouldn't cover his butt. I imagined that before the cleanse began, he would slather lines of yellow, green, and splotches of red on his face from crushed roses, stems, and shrubs. Then he would don a headdress made of bones from animals he had killed and feathers from the papagayo. He would walk barefoot because I thought Indigenous Ecuadorians from the jungle didn't wear shoes. My mom didn't care what he'd look like, just that he would save me.

On a warm night in 2005, Victor drove through the gates of my home on the Ecuadorian coast in a rusted truck from the previous century. I watched him from behind one of the windows, the house's lights illuminating the stamped concrete yard and his tanned skin as he opened the truck's door and walked out wearing jeans and a T-shirt. He looked like my dad, my math tutor, or the chauffeurs who picked up the rich kids from my high school. He had a stout belly, a mustache that spread above his lip, and thick eyebrows that made his forehead look small. He opened the door to the bed of the truck and began hauling bags into our empty living room. I was convinced that he was a con man, bringing utensils to defraud my parents out of their money in an elaborate scheme. I scoffed and followed my mother, her friend Laura, and my brother into our living room. I wanted to burst out with a laugh, but then it dawned on me why Victor was there in the first place. I looked down at my body, seeing how much it had changed in such a short time.

The cleanse started at midnight and ended when the sun rose. A month before Victor visited us, I had lost my appetite for everything except water. My palate didn't want to taste anything. Before then, food was a form of pleasure as well as sustenance. I would be entranced by the tangy smell of cooked ceviche—a lemon-based concoction with fish, shrimp, and other seafood seeped in curative powers tailored for the hungover but with equally restorative magic for the sober. Suddenly all ceviche did was trigger my tongue to gag in disgust. Not just ceviche, everything. When the smell of just-cooked chicharrón engulfed my room from the kitchen downstairs, my stomach hurled bile toward my esophagus.

I didn't know it then—who could?—but my body had shut down.

Within the span of a year and a half, I had moved from Norwalk, Connecticut, to the small town I was born in:

Milagro, Ecuador. I had gotten on the plane against my will. For a decade, from the ages of five until I was fifteen, Norwalk had been my home. The reason my family moved back to Ecuador was simple. In my hometown of Milagro, my paternal grandfather had gotten sick; my father didn't want to abandon him. But not even five months after our move, my grandfather died—and my father began an affair. I had to learn how to read and write in my first language, a tongue I hardly spoke outside the walls of my home when I had lived in Connecticut. The culture shock rippled through my body like the Ecuadorian earthquakes I would experience. I fell in love with a boy who liked but fake-loved me for eight months.

And that—teenage heartbreak—was the tipping point.

By the time Victor the Shaman entered the gates of my home, my father had returned to the United States—unable to financially support us in Ecuador—and my mother felt she had no other option but to call on a man with supernatural powers to fix me. Sprinkle in some mourning then add some homesickness, a dash of confusion about what "home" really meant, plus a sliver of screaming parental fights, and a smidge of a broken heart. My mind and my body had endured too much and just shut down, starting with my stomach.

"Mija, you never leave any food," my mom had complained as she grabbed my plate from the dining room table just a few weeks before. Her warm eyes had given me a puzzled look. I made her confusion disappear when I asked her to save it for the following day.

The following day became the day after, the day after became a week; suddenly a week became three weeks, and all I could manage to eat were bites of cheese, a strawberry, and a papaya here and there. But nothing cooked, nothing soaked in oil, nothing from an animal. I could bear none of this. By the third week my mother entered my bedroom and sat on the edge of my bed as I lay under the blue-flowered blanket.

"I know you're sad, mija. Nothing has been easy. And this whole Carlos bit . . . ," she said as she placed her hand on my shoulder then slowly tucked a strand of hair behind my ear. My mother had always been skinny, but she ate as much as my burly father did—sometimes much more. She was pretty in an effortless way. She didn't need to brush her hair in the mornings, and her sparkly straight teeth had been created by her genes, not fixed by metal braces. Her skin was shades lighter than the tanned hue my dad and I shared. People had often remarked that we looked like cousins or sisters, not mother and daughter.

"You have to eat. Real food. You'll have no butt by the end of the month," she said as her voice went from worried to a slight tease. I chuckled weakly.

"I'll try," I said.

It wasn't that I hadn't been trying. I tried to stop breathing so I couldn't smell the beef full of adobo. The aroma and tastes of my mother's, relatives', and even strangers' food had always been a source of great pleasure throughout my life. Refusing to eat was not a cognizant decision. One of Ecuador's comforts was the variety of food I had eaten with gusto. There was the lady with the kiosk on a main street in my hometown that sold tripita, small cow intestine. She had been at the same intersection for decades and even recognized my father—whom she hadn't seen in years—when he took me to eat there the first time. I sat on the shaky plastic red chairs placed on the sidewalk, while the sun set and the equatorial heat began to wane and the town's residents zip-zapped around me on motorcycles, bicycles, and scooters. I rolled my eyes at the families of four on small bikes then gasped when I saw one of the kids cradling a baby in her arms. Constant beeps from taxi cabs interrupted the conversations buzzing around us. The nearby buses barely stopped to let people off, and their almost-halts flung dust everywhere. My father joked that the intestines' tasty flavor was born from that dust.

When I stopped eating, it never crossed my mind that this would bring Carlos back, or my grandfather back, or my father back. But disgust had overpowered me the day I was dumped as fast as ignited fuel burns through a shard of wood. The smell of cooked meat triggered a gagging frenzy. I couldn't bear to mix beans and rice together on a spoon and raise it to my mouth.

Heartbreak should be called bodybreak.

Sleep permitted some semblance of peace. The bed was a cocoon where my body and mind waded into a tolerable absence of consciousness. My escape began in the evening, after I got back from high school to do the assigned homework for the day, and then I slept until the alarm rang the following day. Some days I woke up at night to drink some water or played with dinner until I asked to be excused. Some nights I refused even this.

After weeks of this ritual, a friend forced me out of bed on a Saturday. At his stoop, while we ignored the street dogs who begged for food, he asked me, too kindly, whether I knew I had forgotten his birthday. I apologized and told him that the days were out of whack, just like me. Still, even as I said sorry, I couldn't wait to hurry across town, get into bed, and enjoy a catatonic state of solace.

People noticed. One day at school, a friend grabbed my arm and inspected it like a bug picked off the floor. "You'll disappear soon," she said. I shrugged her comment off the same way I did whenever someone asked if I was hungry. But I noticed too. My jeans were looser around my thighs, and my hipbones protruded more than before. I could knock on them with my knuckles. My large eyes bulged out like my face was a skeleton. But I was convinced that once the pain went away, my body surely would make space for appetite.

One day my mom stomped into my room, the wooden floor shaking with each step. She no longer sat on the edge of the bed or caressed my hair. She stood over me, arms crossed, anger replacing the sympathy her eyes had previously shown me. The curves of her lips faded away when she was angry, and on that night they'd formed one tight, pursed line.

"You need to eat. You're almost seventeen. Do you want me to force-feed you as if you were a baby?" Each word she blurted out became louder and louder. I resisted the urge to pull the covers over my face. "Because I will. I will make you sit down and eat every last drop. You better get it together because I don't want that, and sure as hell you don't either." She trudged out of my room and I pulled the covers over my face, forcing myself into the nothingness of sleep.

I was secretly happy my dad wasn't there—he would have demanded that I stop the bullshit, as he surely would have called it.

One day I woke up, spread my arms up to yawn, and saw a circle on my left bicep. Its width was bigger than a golf ball but smaller than a tennis ball—a crusty scab, or what would remain of a charred forest after a fire. I had not gotten a cut or a scrape, especially not one that looked like a perfect circle. If I pulled off the scab, what would be below? Tiny worms or gray pus? I prodded but felt the pseudo-scab rooted to my skin. I went crying to my mother and demanded to be taken to a doctor.

We saw three doctors that day. The first one was a self-taught dermatologist who inspected a book as she looked at my arm. She read out loud different skin infections and stared at me like I would know what I had if only I heard it. The next doctor told me he didn't know what it was and to see someone else. The third did a skin biopsy with a utensil that punched into my skin and took a few millimeters of the crusty scab. There were no worms or pus below, but dark blood dripped from the intentional wound; the sample was sent to a laboratory for testing.

If sleep had been my only comfort, I now began to fear closing my eyes. Maybe a perfect scabby circle would appear on my right arm, below my navel, or on a thigh when I woke up. My skin could become a mix of fish scales the color of coal. I no longer obsessively replayed what I had done wrong with Carlos; now I worried that I'd acquired some terminal illness that would rot my skin. I woke up in the middle of a dream where I was standing in front of a mirror with my entire body covered with a bruise that had overtaken even the skin of my lips.

A pained heart I could tolerate, but I couldn't withstand being disgusted by everything *and* having putrid skin. Three days later, the results were ready. The dermatologist's office was painted in an old yellow, and there were no windows. He sat at a mahogany desk, probably almost as old as he was; white, gray, and black hairs sprouted on his eyebrows. He didn't wear a white coat, just black pants and a dull green shirt. I felt like he lived in his seat, especially with the tip of his belly touching the edge of the desk.

"Sometimes stress makes our body react in weird ways," he said. "Just like hives appear when you get nervous, the immune system acts up with too much stress. Are you anemic? Are you eating well?"

"It's been more than a month now. She's just been eating snacks, doctor. Not real food," my mother said as she side-eyed me.

"If you want that to go away, you *must* eat," he said, pointing to my arm. "Take this medicine, put on this cream, and eat," he added as he slid a prescription toward my mother. If the spot didn't leave or another one sprouted up, I would need to see him again.

As we left the doctor to get into our red truck, my mother called her friend Laura.

"What do I do? How can I make her pain stop?" she asked. I rolled my eyes then felt guilty when tears streamed down her face, disrupting the thick layers of mascara she never left the house without applying.

"Okay, okay; I'll do anything at this point. Anything."

My mother decided on a limpia, a cleansing to cease the tears, to sterilize the pustules on my epidermis, and to stop the unwelcome regurgitation, the hunger pains ravaging my stomach.

Victor strode into my living room and opened a bag of rocks, positioning them on an expansive sheet on our living room floor. Some rocks were lumpy; others looked sanded and smooth. Few had stubbles that perked up in blue and green when the light glistened off them. Light easily trespassed through a few moonstones. One thick rock gleamed like the black of my progressively healing scab. In the middle of all the rocks stuck out a slightly rusted sword. It wasn't thin enough to be used for fencing or thick enough for battle. My brother was enthralled by the sword's purple handle and asked Victor if he could pick it up.

"If you can," he told him. His voice was as deep as the crater of a centuries-old volcano.

While Victor set up the area where the cleansing would take place, my slender ten-year-old brother reached for the sword to prove the shaman wrong. He could barely get the handle off the floor, and announced that it probably weighed as much as he did. The man let him admire the blunted edge for a few minutes. He placed bedsheets on the living room's wide windows to keep the light out. The sofas had been removed to the spacious dining room, but we kept the seat cushions and pillows to sit on. My feet were on the cool floor, but my legs and butt were comfortable on a pillow. The adobe-colored walls looked pale and naked, with the television remaining as the only pre-cleansing furniture. I had a full view of the rock altar while he moved around and positioned them like he was working on a puzzle. When he finished, he left for a few minutes to use the bathroom and returned barefoot and dressed all in white. White shorts and a tank top. No headdress made from the feathers of the papagayo.

Victor had requested that we wear white clothes too. Did this also include panties? I had looked through my cabinets but found only pink, blue-striped, perky purple panties—my sixteen-year-old version of appropriate underwear. To be on the safe side, I wore white sweatpants, a white bra, a white T-shirt, and no panties.

Victor sat with his back to the altar of rocks and faced us.

"Before we start, I want to say that this is not magic. I have a gift that was granted to me by my ancestors."

Laura went first because she'd had a cleansing with Victor before. My brother was already fast asleep in between my mother and me.

"Make sure that you don't cross your fingers or arms. Your bodies have to be open," he said. He turned off the light, sat in an upright position with the balls of his feet touching, and began to utter unintelligible words. I sat intrigued, my eyes getting used to the lack of light. I could see the outline of his body, but I couldn't make out his expressions in the darkness.

After Victor's guttural sounds ceased, he and Laura began to converse, almost like an interview. The questions sounded more like demands, and each time after Laura spoke, he let the information linger, letting seconds pass before responding.

"What are you worried about?" he said.

"I always worry about my daughter. She's in Spain without me, and that was the best decision . . . but I still worry about her. What she's doing, who she's with, school, everything."

Every family I knew had at least one relative who was living outside the country. Laura's case was an exception because her daughter, Carla, was my age, and Laura supported her with what she earned in Ecuador. My dad was in the United States, supporting us on a garbage man's salary. That he was working in another country to make sure I was fed weighed on my psyche, especially now that I weighed less than a hundred pounds.

"I can sense that your daughter is doing well. She'll be successful," he said. I processed each of his words hesitantly. I wasn't convinced that he had any powers, but it wasn't the appropriate moment to voice my concerns. After all, he was my mother's last recourse.

They continued to go back and forth, more than an hour of conversation, until Victor told Laura she'd see her daughter soon and that she would leave Ecuador earlier than she had expected. This left her at ease, and I wondered what "soon" meant to Victor. When he was almost done with Laura, she asked him to cleanse her daughter. He got up, faced the rocks and began chanting. The only word I understood was "Carla." He didn't shuffle his feet or move around in a circle. He just raised his hand in front of him, toward the rocks, toward the roof as he muttered garbled words and chants. But they sounded confident, as if someone in a different language was speaking on the phone with a relative and giving unintelligible directions in a hasty manner. I felt a surge of coldness creep over my body, even though there was no wind, even though no windows were open. We heard sounds come from outside the house—a motorcycle revving, a drunk man wailing a song, dogs fighting in the street. I wished I had brought a blanket, but I reminded myself that I couldn't dare venture into sleep.

It was my turn next.

"How are you?" he asked me.

"I'm okay. I could be better."

"And how could you be better?" he asked. It was so dark I couldn't see his face, but his voice, deep and determined, flooded the room. I grabbed the soft pillow below me and held on so tightly I was sure the nail marks would be etched in the fabric forever. It was too warm for a blanket, but suddenly I wanted to hide under my bed cover and get swallowed by its softness.

"I haven't really felt hungry lately."

"And why is that?"

"Because my boyfriend and I . . . we broke up."

It felt ridiculous and embarrassing even as I said it, but not even embarrassment had made me eat. I waited for him to say the same things my family and friends had: "You're too good for him." "He doesn't even have a car." "You'll forget about him soon." "In a few years you'll remember this and laugh." "Get over it." Not getting over him meant that I was weak. I waited for Victor to ask me details, but he never asked about the breakup.

"You have a lot going on in your head."

"Yes. Maybe," I said, not knowing how to respond.

"Tell me about the ring."

"Ring? Like a ring you wear on your finger?"

"Yes. That ring you can't stop thinking about."

Maybe my mother had said something. It wasn't a secret in my family what I had done. Many years ago, my grandfather had given me a gold ring. It was thick and wide, and the head was one flat line divided into two parts. On one side my initials appeared, "VB"; on the other, four engraved squares surrounded a small rock. It was my most prized possession; my favorite gift from my grandfather. But I had made a stupid mistake, one I would regret for the rest of my life. In the weeks leading up to the move from the United States to Ecuador, I gave my ring to Lucas, my neighbor and maybe boyfriend, as a promise that we would see each other again and that he would give it back. After I moved to Ecuador, my grandfather died swiftly. At that point I just wanted my ring back. But when I reached out to Lucas, he told me it had gotten lost. My father didn't scream, but he was disappointed and swore that he'd never gift me a ring for the rest of my life. He'll keep that promise. This object, not much in monetary value, one I had thought would end up on my finger, will forever be lost. It will always be a sign of my gullibility and how hard I had clung to the belief that I would soon be back in the United States. I didn't want to tell this story in depth, so I told Victor the short version.

"I see," he said. "The only thing you can do is ask your grandfather for forgiveness."

"I wish I could. He passed away."

"You can still ask your abuelo for forgiveness. He's always taking care of you, and he knows. Don't let it weigh on you too much, okay?"

"Bueno," I said.

I wanted a breather, to drink some water, curl my body into a tiny ball, and fall asleep. I wanted to get away from the memories, the shaman in my house, and my mother's desperateness. But Victor had another plan.

"Did something happen in a basement?"

It wasn't a question but an attempt to pry information, and after the last word was uttered he began to cough. I had a feeling it was just a way to buy me some time. I was glad we were cloaked in darkness, because my eyes widened in shock. There was no way he could know what happened in that basement. It was the only secret I had kept from my mother, my father, the world—sometimes I hid the secret from myself. The only other person who knew what happened was thousands of miles away, and he would never reveal what he had done.

Victor was more than a shaman; I was convinced he was a medium. I had buried, almost eliminated, this experience from the memories of my life. This was not something I wanted to discuss with my mother, Laura, and an all-seeing shaman.

"I don't want to talk about that."

"Does your mother know?"

"No."

"She's never told me about a basement," my mother said. I could feel her trying to look at me. My face burned in fear. I didn't want to say more. I didn't want to face something with others that I hadn't even faced myself. I held onto the tears because I didn't want my cries to be the only thing heard in the silence of night. It seemed that Victor felt my fear and quickly asked me another question. I was thankful, and I hoped my mother would never ask me what had happened. I wanted to believe I would one day be ready to tell her that story.

"What happened to your arm?" Victor asked.

"The doctor says it's all the stress. It should be going away soon," I said.

"I see. Victoria, will you let me connect to your body so I can see what's wrong? I need your permission," he said.

"Yes," I said. I tried not to crisscross my limbs. Every time my hands lifted from the warm pillow beneath my butt—so I could hug my shoulders as if I had just been dragged out of a cold shower—I remembered that I couldn't cross them. I wanted my body to undo itself. *Remain open, remain open, remain open,* I told myself.

He told us to wait a few minutes while he connected to my body. He began to hum, and after some time his stomach began to pulse up and down. I couldn't see it, but I heard him burp, cough, and try to contain belches before he bellowed in pain. I felt nothing and wished that I could somehow sense the connection.

"Ayayai, niña, this pain that you're in. . . . How do you . . . take it? It burns . . . ," he trailed off and began to breathe loud enough that the inhalation through his nose and exhalation through his mouth was all we could hear. A puff out, and a shaky breath in. When he was about to say something, burps thwarted his efforts.

"Is this . . . how you feel right now?" he asked in a low voice.

I believed that he felt my pain. He knew what was inside my head and inside my body. For a moment, I was content that someone else could feel it. I was pleased that my mom and her friend could see that I wasn't lying. I was taken aback by all the memories of the last couple of years I had stored away. The ring, the basement, my grandfather, Carlos, my dad. Some of these were hidden, but they lay dormant inside me.

And that's when I realized that maybe Carlos was just the last thing to undo me.

"I have to get out. It's too much," he muttered.

He hummed again, and the burps made fewer and fewer interruptions until heavy sighs took over. Once the pain departed, he began to speak.

"I know it hurts to be abandoned. But you're going to destroy your stomach if you don't eat."

"I know," I said. The last bit I'd heard many times before.

"Victoria, do you love yourself?"

The question took me by surprise. Of course I did. Everyone loved themselves, just the way you automatically love a brother or sister. Because that is simply how it is.

"Yes," I replied.

"Would someone who loves herself not eat?"

I remained silent in the darkness.

"Sometimes we love others more than we love ourselves. We can give love, but it's hard for us to keep it and show it to ourselves."

No one had talked to me like this. It's not something I had ever thought about. But I knew, as he asked me, that I had no love to offer anyone.

"What's your name?" Victor said.

"Victoria."

"What does Victoria mean? It means "victory." And victory means that you overcome challenges. Your name already embodies it. Now *you* have to embody it. You're already a victory. Live up to it."

"Gracias," I said.

"Remember your name."

"Okay."

My mother went next. She talked about my father, my brother, and me. Everything but herself. And I felt selfish as I heard her speak. I had disappointed her, even though she never said it. She just wanted me to eat like I used to, to gain weight, to stop crying. I'd gone from a size two to a double zero in pants. She wondered if I would have become this girl if we had stayed in the United States. I wondered the same. I tried to listen to her entire cleansing, but my mind drifted away.

For the first time in a while, I began to think about me. Not in how sad I felt and how I longed for bed. I thought about what it meant to love myself. How stupid it would be if I gave all my love away to someone who didn't want it. But I was still afraid that my taste buds, throat, and stomach would continue to overpower me. That the sadness would be victorious.

After some time, slivers of light begin to seep through the sheets covering the windows. Before the sun began to consume the land, my mother and I walked outside to our yard. The morning felt cool, enough to send a quick shiver across my spine, but it was still warm enough for a T-shirt. It would only get hotter by the hour, hot enough for the yard's concrete to singe the balls of my feet. Victor walked to his car and returned with a wine bottle in his right hand. He asked me to stand by the gate with specks of rust eating away at the corners—the one I had never seen open since I'd moved back to that house.

"Close your eyes. You'll feel a little bit cold, but the cleansing is almost over."

As the birds chirped in the mango trees, Victor began chanting. Not in Spanish but in a language only he could understand. His voice became a song, strong enough to be heard at a stadium. Long vowels weaved into one another, short whoops and guttural sounds rang from his throat. I had my eyes closed, and just as I opened them, he brought the bottle to his lips and sucked the liquid into his mouth. I knew what was coming, and my body tensed as though a soccer ball was being aimed at my head. I closed my eyes before I felt the spray shiver my arms, neck, and face. Liquor made of sugarcane.

We were face to face when the first shower enveloped me. He continued the cleansing ritual by chugging, chanting, and spraying as he circled me. Goose bumps erupted all over my body. The smell was strong but sweet. All my senses were on edge and waiting for the next slap of liquor on my skin. When he was behind me, I peeked out of one eye and saw my mother in front of me, hands clasped in prayer. A face devoid of makeup, sleepy, worried, but with a flicker of hope. I wanted to know what he was saying, whether he was reciting a sacred prayer that his ancestors had passed down to him or if these words were new, different, based on the singular issues of each person that he met. When it was done, I was left shaking.

"You can change your clothes, but don't shower until after you've slept. Vamos. Let your body absorb this."

My mother's turn was next, and this time I kept my eyes open when he heaved the liquor from his mouth. His eyes were closed while he reached inside to belt out his chant. Victor only opened them when it was time to hold and spew the liquor from his mouth. My mother shivered before it hit her, and she let out a surprised squeal every time another part of her body got wet. The sun was completely out by then, and the sounds beyond the gates and walls began to evolve. Car brakes squeaked, the metal roll-up doors clanged as local businesses opened for the day, and the smell of soft bread from the bakery surrounded the neighborhood.

Once he was finished with us, he announced that he was not yet done with the house. I walked back to my room and stared at him from the window. In the yard, he lit a match to palo santo while he continued to chant. He raised the wood in his right hand, the burning end almost touching the cement walls of our house. His face didn't look gaunt like mine, but just as it had when he'd arrived. He spread the smoke by the outside sink, both gates, the two gardens, around each of the mango trees, and the area fenced off with mosquito nets where we held gatherings.

By the time he was done, my eyelids struggled to remain open. But I fought sleep until he entered the house, and then he began burning something else. I changed into dry clothes, but my hair was damp with the liquor's spice. I put on my pajamas, and the odor of jasmine emerged through the wooden floors, soothing me and urging me to rest. My mother's room was just across from mine, and it had dark window shades to keep out the new day's light. I crept under the covers, and the liquor began to seep from my hair onto the pillow. Before I fell asleep, I heard a knock on the door.

"Buenas noches y buenos días. No need to worry, you'll be fine," Victor said as he lifted the curled leaves to the corners of the room. The front of his white shirt had damp spots from the sugarcane liquor, and he remained alert, like the night before hadn't happened. I replied with a good night, and then he left the room. In that moment, like so many in those past weeks, sleep beat hunger. I resisted all thoughts except for relishing the jasmine engulfing my nostrils, convinced that this was what peace smelled like. As I closed my eyes, I vowed to remember to love myself more than I loved anyone else. And I whispered, *Victoria, victory, Victoria, victory*, lulling myself into a dreamless sleep.

HOW TO BE AN ECUADORIAN GIRL

You learn to replace peanut butter and jelly sandwiches, fries, and sloppy joes with decadent fruits. Mangoes first because you don't have to leave the house to savor them, even though they wake you up with bangs on the zinc roof in the middle of the night. You learn that sapote is your favorite—a plump sphere, brown lining on the outside filled with a bright orange gunk, succulent and sweet, which gets stuck to the spaces between your teeth. Guaba is another treat you beg your uncle to bring when he comes home from work. It's a long and skinny enclosure of flexible green bark. The only edible part is the lining of the seeds inside: white, fuzzy, and savory. You learn when the vendor who sells ciruelas from a rickety cart usually stops by your street. They look like tiny mangoes but taste nothing like them. At first you're not sure how you like them: red and ripe or green and citrusy. You decide there is no point in choosing, because you will devour both.

Victoria Buitron

Your mother tells you that you must never forget this is not the Yoni. "Be careful with those short-shorts," she says. But it's hot enough that spools of sweat form as soon as you get out of the shower, as you get out of bed, as you walk a few feet to the corner store. You learn that those shorts aren't just shorts. They will define you; the vecinos will whisper to one another. You will be the gringa slut who doesn't know that fifteen-year-old girls can't dress in shorts on the streets because men will acknowledge it. You wear jeans that stick to your legs like gooey face masks. It's hot, and taking them off feels like pulling tinfoil from leftovers. But you learn that shorts are a message—to strangers, to relatives, to neighbors—that your parents don't want you to send.

You ask why you live in Ecuador but use currency from the United States. They tell you the shortened version: The economy collapsed a few years ago and the sucre, the currency used from the 1880s until 2000, became worthless. Ecuador adopted US dollars. Out of all the currencies in the world, somehow they chose that one instead of the neighboring sol from Peru or the peso from Colombia. A relief, because learning a conversion rate would have been annoying. All around you people sell fruits, ice cream, and a taxi ride for just a dollar or less. The bus from Milagro to Guayaquil is only ninety cents. Everywhere you hear dólar, dólar, dólar.

You accept there is a different type of poverty in your hometown. There are fewer beggars than the ones at the highway exits back in Connecticut. But children your brother's age, even younger, sell candy, cigarettes, and lollipops. Have they ever stepped inside a school? Who taught them how to add and subtract? Did they have to do conversion rates when they were six years old with their parents help a few years ago? They walk behind their parents, or alone, in front of banks with lines of humans surrounding the block, hoping someone has a craving for gum. The pitch of their voices goes up so that they sound younger than they actually are. At first it shocks you that the corner stores in your neighborhood are manned by kids younger than you. Then it becomes another facet of life in Milagro. In this small town, everyone works, even children.

Some people in Ecuador, you learn, are filthy rich. An enclave of the rich separate themselves from the poor by a river and bridge. You pass by Durán, always in construction, where the gutters are open for weeks on end. It's a town on the side of the highway covered in a gray coating of concrete. Across the bridge, to the right, is Samborondón. Gated communities, and men with guns are at each entrance. The first time you visit, you think of Florida. Lines of palms trees, malls on each side, and a sudden rare gringo sighting: McDonald's. The first time you visit, you hear an accent you've never heard before. It sounds like the tone of superiority. You'll learn this is called speaking with a potato in the mouth. Hablar con la papa en la boca. The accent of the rich. This is where you will go to school. You will traverse between your small town, about an hour away, cross Yaguachi, then Durán, and arrive in Samborondón because your padre promised your madre that history would not repeat itself. You have no idea what it means to be the other, yet.

You learn to incorporate phrases into your vocabulary. The first one that clicks is "pueblo chico, infierno grande." "Small town, big hell." One day, after you're done listening in on classrooms in Spanish at a local school in Milagro, you walk home with a friend. He has his left hand over your shoulders and you walk side by side. He is not your boyfriend. You will never kiss him; you have no plans to do so. When you get home, your mom already knows who you were with at 3:37 p.m. Her uncle called to let her know. Your mom tells him, "So what?" She knows he's your friend. But she still tells you: "You see, this is what it means to live in a small town. There are no secrets." Your dad then tells you he has eyes everywhere and will always know your whereabouts. You shrug because you don't care. But the gringa in you is annoyed because everyone minded their own business in the Yoni.

The next phrase you learn is "los trapos sucios se lavan en casa." "Wash your dirty clothes at home." You realize this isn't completely true. They are washed at home, but people hang their trapos to dry because there are no drying machines. Washed panties are put out on clotheslines for everyone to see. Neighbors can't help but peek. The phrase is a lie your parents and ancestors made up to pretend they believe no one knows what goes on inside other people's houses. But everyone knows. You say hi, give the customary kiss on the cheek to someone your age you just meet. He leaves and then someone tells you that the poor kid doesn't know the father that raised him isn't his biological father. They even know the name of his biological dad. "How do you know his business?" you ask. "Vox populi," the person says. "Voice of the people." Popular opinion. Gossip. You feel bad for the kid, his trapos are dirty, and he doesn't even know it.

You speak to people who have been separated from their mothers, fathers, sisters, brothers by an ocean, or a tourist visa, or a residency petition that continues to elude them. That could have been you if you weren't partly a gringa. If your mom had not been born as what some deem to be an anchor baby. If your father had arrived like many of his friends to the United States and overstayed their tourist visas. But you learn you are lucky because your two passports mean you've lived with your parents almost your whole life. You do not wait for Sunday to buy calling cards to speak to your mother for an hour. You don't wait for the father you haven't seen in eight years to send you brand-label clothing from Italy. You don't live with a slew of uncles and aunts. Your father is gone, but you know decades won't pass before you see him again. You do not pray for a visa to see a mother you haven't touched since you were three years old. You learn the privilege of a US passport.

You see your skin for the first time. You learn the phrase "mejorar la raza." "Better the race." It means "whiten the race," but the people that say it avoid the words "white" and "black." Girls and women want blonde hair. You learn that white skin is coveted. You are not white, and your hair is not straight. You learn to whiten the hairs on your arms with products you buy at the pharmacy. Lightening the hairs makes your skin look whiter. You've never felt ugly until now. The nickname of a girl just a shade darker than you, with hair the same color and texture, is negra. "Black." This is her nickname. You ask: "But why?" Everyone just tells you that she is, indeed, Black. Your gringa mind wonders why it's OK for someone's nickname to be "Black." She seems okay with it. Happy, even. But it makes you uncomfortable. You don't know it then, but this is just the beginning of learning about one of the remnants of colonialism: the adulation toward those who are white and blonde.

The most intriguing phrase you learn is "domingo siete." "Seven Sundays?" "Seventh Sunday?" "Sunday the Seventh?" You wonder how to translate this into English the first time you hear it. You think about God resting on the seventh day. But it turns out this phrase means "unplanned pregnancy." God, Jesus, and the Virgin Mary. The seventh day. Your mom arrived with her seventh Sunday a month after she turned eighteen. A relative tells you someone said you would surely follow in the steps of your mother. You remind yourself to make sure history doesn't repeat itself.

Sundays are not for church or silence.

They are for visiting the grave of your abuelos.

Eating the raspados, shaved ice drenched in gooey condensed milk and flavored in a thick syrupy liquid, outside the cemetery. They are for eating on the concrete yard, watching the latest fútbol game on television.

You learn to live with dozens of relatives nearby. They live within a mile, two miles, three miles. You hear their voices through the wooden floors while you wake on Sunday mornings. Each weekend your yard, your house, is teeming with relatives. Drinking beer. Eating cangrejos. Hosting a barbecue. In a family of eight uncles, with four living close by, parties and reunions are the norm. On Sundays you lie on the hammock and gossip with your cousins while the salsa music plays in the background from another corner of the yard.

You hate conjugating verbs in Spanish, such as "like": gustar. It makes your mind do leaps. Él me gusta. Yo le gusto. At first you can't differentiate between how to say, "I like him" and "He likes me." Somehow, gustar is an anomaly, and you have to conjugate it differently than other verbs. No one can explain why. The language is what it is. This was your first language, but it's not the language you've used outside your house for the last decade. People make fun of your slight gringa accent. People laugh when you can't say a word correctly. People try to guess the word you can't remember. You still dream in English, but just as sluggishly as you learn to put diacritical marks on Spanish words, you increase the command of your first language in real life and in your dreams. You slowly embody a full-fledged ecuatoriana, but she's still different from the girl you would have become if you had never left.

BLOOD IS THICKER
THAN MANGO JUICE

On Saturday, August 21, 2004, my mother, brother, and I left for Ecuador. It was my father's decision to leave everything for his father, my abuelo, Reinaldo, a decision he made for all of us, even my dog. When we arrived to the airport and I saw Sleepy, my black Labrador retriever, disappear inside his kennel on the conveyor belt, I began to cry. Throughout the check-in process and the security gate, I could not stop crying. I was secretly happy my father wouldn't be joining us; he stayed in Connecticut for a few more weeks to finish up some paperwork. Before we said goodbye, he had already pleaded with me to stop crying. I couldn't tell whether it was because he was embarrassed or if he finally realized how devastated I felt. I knew that we didn't abandon family members. We aren't gringos. We don't leave our fathers and mothers in a home and pay for strangers to take care of them, but I didn't think this meant we would deviate the trajectory of our lives altogether. I wanted to be selfish and say, *What about me? Why is my grandfather's life more important than mine?* But I knew I had to keep my mouth shut.

"¿Por qué lloras?" my father asked me. The space between his eyebrows was tight and made two small lumps while he stared at the tears flowing from my eyes. "What? Is it Lucas? Is that why you're crying?" he asked. I said yes just to get him to stop speaking. I didn't tell him that I didn't want a new life, in a new place, in a place that was more of a pueblo than an actual city, in a country they had deliberately taken me away from when I couldn't speak in complete sentences.

When I boarded the plane, I forced myself to sleep, to escape, until our arrival in my homeland. I woke up some minutes before we landed. By the time the tires touched the runway, the flight attendants avoided looking at me. Between sobs, as my chest heaved, I gasped for air. I was being forced to leave at the ripe age of checking for pimples. Junior just stared at me and my tears. He was only nine. As long as my mother and his toys were there, he had left nothing behind.

In the heart of Milagro was a church with a steeple that rose well above the surrounding buildings. In front of it was a park, or the Ecuadorian definition of a park: a concrete square with a few benches where drunk men congregated and women avoided at night. Milagro, in an effort to modernize, became awash with gray, and there was hardly any grass in sight. The rest of the town was littered with hardware stores; liquor stores; schools;

homes that sold coconut, vanilla, and chocolate ice cream; pharmacies; warehouses filled with bootleg CDs and movies for a dollar each; cybers or computer stations connected to the internet. The abandoned rail line that cut through the town served as the spot for vendors to perch their kiosks. Throughout the day on Sundays, the town's residents would visit the cemetery where some of my ancestors from my paternal and maternal lines rest aboveground in fraying concrete vaults.

About an hour after we left the airport in Guayaquil, we arrived at the house where my father had grown up—a mansion in the middle of a poor neighborhood—followed by a caravan of cousins, uncles, and my parents' friends. This was my abuelo's house, and where I'd spent my life until I was five years old. The neighborhood is called Bellavista, "beautiful view" in Italian. But there was hardly a beautiful view when I arrived. Only the avenue that led to our front gate was paved. The surrounding streets were just dirt. A sawmill stood across from the house, and I would soon feel mini earthquakes from the force of heavy logs dumped on the earth. Half of the block on which our house stood was owned by my grandfather. In the 1970s the space had been one of the few movie theaters Milagro had. By the early 2000s the area had been divided into small sections and rented out. One was a small corner store, another was a restaurant that sold rotisserie chicken, and the other was a butcher shop. When I had visited in past years, my uncles had made it clear that I couldn't go past the butcher shop. I was not to walk farther down the street unless I was accompanied by them or another male relative. Tío Pedro, who had lived with my abuelo all the years my father was away, assured me that I would be pickpocketed, or worse, if I ever ventured down the street. The municipality didn't even bother paving the street beyond our block.

The home's main door stood in the corner, carved into a white metal gate that rose twelve feet. It was attached to beige walls of the same height on both ends, creating a large four-walled box secluding us from the world. Shattered beer bottles shone on top of the walls and glistened like rubies in the piercing sun. They were spread across the top of all the walls to cut robbers who attempted to scale them. When the gates opened, I gazed at the house I'd be living in. A yard the size of two basketball fields, two small gardens at each side of the gate with coconut trees and agave plants, and tall mango trees full of mini dinosaur–looking iguanas. The five mango trees filled the sky, shading half the yard. The two-story home was large enough for my abuelo, my Tío Pedro and his wife, my mother, my father, my brother, and me. The house boasted five bedrooms, six inside bathrooms, and a bathroom at an enclosed area in the yard for outside gatherings, of which there would be many. Behind the trees stood a house that took the shape of the letter *L*; two walls with a beige facade connected in a 90-degree angle. Windows, each one of them with intricate white bars, lined both walls. That house was the result of my grandfather's businesses and money my father had sent from the United States.

When the car stopped, the first thing I did was ask for Sleepy be taken out of the kennel. When I went to see him, rheum was bulging from his eyes. He had been crying in the cargo storage of the plane. Everyone was afraid of the big black dog and stood back when he was freed. "Be careful with Robert!" I said. Robert, a black-and-white dog that Tío Pedro had bought from a drunk man for ten cents a few years before, was the dog of the house, owner of the yard. His real name was Rover, but no one could pronounce it without adding a *t* at the end.

Sleepy ran off to smell his new home, his new country. He leapt from one mango tree to another, then to the gardens by the entrance of the house. He sniffed the cobblestones, surely confused that there was no grass. Soon Sleepy noticed the other dog. Robert had only shared this house with humans, and the intruder made the hair on the nape of his neck frazzle up. He leapt, announcing that this territory was his, and both dogs bared their fangs. They hurtled on the ground, paws grazing the air through growls and yaps. I hoped they wouldn't kill each other.

"They have to get to know each other. A quick fight and they'll be friends," Tío Freddy said. He was the eldest brother of my father's eight half-siblings. His hair poofed out in tight curls, and his stomach strained against the shirt he wore.

After a few seconds of tumbling and barking, Tío Pedro scolded his dog. "¡Ya, Robert, ya! Sleeper is your new friend!"

As the dogs eyed each other from different corners of the yard, I finally spotted my grandfather.

His gray, almost blue eyes struck me. He had made his way slowly to greet us outside. I hadn't seen him in about two years, but his body had changed drastically. His arms were missing the meat that had once filled them, and his skin hung loose like a rooster's wattle. He took each step as if walking on ice, careful not to slip, making sure that his bones were still strong enough to hold him up. I could see more of his scalp than the gray hairs he always slicked back with a comb. His jaw was sturdy, but his semi-plump cheeks were losing weight and the skin on his arms had old and new bruises—some the color of red wine—from blood tests, I was sure. My abuelo's body was betraying him, and he needed the help of machines to do what my body could do by itself. He hugged and kissed all of us.

"Mija, ¿cómo estuvo el vuelo?" he said. He embraced me, and as he finished giving me a hug, he lowered his forehead to hit it with mine. Just a swift nudge, what he had always done when I was a kid to say hi or goodbye. A cocacho, he called it. His scent, the same husky cologne he used when I could barely walk, reached my nostrils. He smelled like how the earth smells in just-born sunlight a few minutes after a swift morning rain. We stared at each other for a few seconds while I took in the new lines and blotches on his face. His eyes thanked me for being there, and I knew I couldn't break his heart with more tears. His body was already being broken.

I never saw my abuelo undergo dialysis. Every few days my uncles, and eventually my father, would take him an hour away to a clinic in Guayaquil where a machine would do what his kidneys couldn't do anymore. The waste, salt, and extra water from his body were removed. The nurses would look for a vein and poke so much he'd always come back home with more bruises.

This allowed him to stay alive, but he came home more disheartened every time. My grandfather could no longer take pleasure in eating food or drinking water. He drank limited amounts of water per day. Maybe if he lived somewhere else, it wouldn't have been as painful, but the heat of the coast forced everyone to drink more water than usual. What the cook served him during breakfast, lunch, and dinner were not the same dishes we had the pleasure of eating. None of his food could have salt, pepper, or any sort of seasoning. The lack of flavor tortured my grandfather, whose life joys had always been thick ribs drowned in juicy gunk, pork chops with a mix of herbs, encebollado drenched in bacalao and salt, plus pitchers of mineral water. Now he was forced to eat yams and greens. He sighed while we ate, staring only at his plate so his mouth wouldn't water if he glanced at another dish.

My father became his daily companion. He arrived in September, and by the following month he had placed my grandfather's bed on the first floor to prevent him from falling down the stairs. They sat on chairs in the yard and talked for hours. I had been taught not to interrupt elders while they spoke, so I hardly ever heard what they discussed. I peeked out of my second-floor window; my father's eyes were solemn, while my grandfather stared at the trees in the yard, trying to ignore a monologue in which my father urged him to continue dialysis.

In early November I heard my abuelo call out to my father from his room.

"Mijo, mijo. Rey. ¡Mijo!"

I walked down the stairs and headed to his room as if he were calling me. My father came out of his room worried, with the phone in hand to call a doctor.

"Quédate aquí," he ordered, with a finger pointed at my face to show he was serious. I stayed. I stood by the windows, knowing I wasn't supposed to look into the other part of the house but hoping I could hear that everything was okay. Abuelo was in such bad shape that he couldn't get up. A few hours later a doctor walked through the gate and my mother told me what happened. His lower torso, including his testicles, had seemed to blow up into a huge water balloon overnight.

"This was actually a good thing," my father told me later that day at our dining room table. "The extra water around his body decided to spread down. If it had traveled up, it might have stopped his heart."

"But is he going to be okay?" I asked.

"Let's hope so, mija. He really has to follow a strict diet. I think he's been drinking more water than he should. It's hard . . . telling him not to drink water. But he's going to have to do it," he said.

Sleepy often tried to run away after we moved into Abuelo's house. The gate had a small door within it that would open with a key or by pressing a button from our living room. The key allowed us to enter the house silently, but each time the button was pressed and a buzz flooded our house, Sleepy saw it as an opportunity to escape from the alien yard. The first time he pushed through someone's legs and shot out, I quickly ran behind him, lucky to have witnessed his escape. By chance, a man was riding on a flimsy carriage with two donkeys leading the way. Sleepy paused his escape to bark at the creatures and raise up on his hind legs to mark his territory. The donkeys kicked, their eyes opened in terror while they tried to flee, and the man cursed while holding on to the lead rope. I felt the eyes of those on the streets, streaming past on bicycles and motorcycles, and heard the gasps of people buying food at the corner store. Sleepy was heavier than I was, and I knew I couldn't stop him. Suddenly Tío Pedro appeared and grabbed Sleepy by his red collar before he could clamp his jaws on the donkeys' hooves.

When my father arrived a few weeks later, he told me that Sleepy had done what he needed to do. "No one would dare come in up the walls and try to enter after seeing that. Word gets around. No one needs to know he's harmless," he said. Sleepy was ferocious toward any other animal but acted like a newborn puppy toward all humans. Still, I was angry that my father hadn't understood my point. Sleepy wasn't running away out of duty but because he didn't know where the hell he had ended up.

I moved back to the coast of Ecuador in the middle of a school year. I would attend Colegio Nuevo Mundo, a private bilingual high school on the outskirts of Guayaquil, when classes started the following school year in April. In order to get familiar with the formal use of Spanish, I also had the opportunity to sit in the classrooms and listen until then, but I didn't want to wake up at five in the morning and travel an hour away. I decided to sit in classrooms of a local school in Milagro while we waited for all the paperwork to go through. During that time, since I had to go to school but had no homework, my grandfather and I spent time together in the yard. I placed a hammock between two mango trees. It cost my abuelo too much energy to lift himself from it, so he preferred to sit in a chair near me. He sat with a sleeveless white T-shirt and thin striped shorts and sandals, with his back hunched into the letter *C*.

He was in physical pain, but I could tell his confinement hurt him the most. For decades he had managed all sorts of businesses. He once had a furniture store and a restaurant side by side on one of Milagro's main streets. He had one movie theater in Milagro and another in a nearby town called Naranjito that he had manned for years. Once he got older, he rented all the spaces out and spent his days visiting his buildings, solving tenants' issues, and overseeing the fruits of the labor that had taken decades of his life.

Now he was surrounded by falling mangoes and his gringa granddaughter. We could hear the life beyond the walls. Every day little earthquakes from the falling trunks across the street shook the walls and trees. The beeps of motorcycles and cabs interrupted our silence. Someone, maybe on our street or a block away, played salsa music at full volume. In Milagro, music was part of life, an expected facet of the neighborhood, a welcome part of the day. Men with kiosks on tires would scream "helaos, helaos, rico helaos" urging people to come out, get some ice cream and relief from the constant heat.

I wish I could say that I took those moments to ask my abuelo questions about his life. I could have asked him how he went from being a tailor to owning a movie theater. I wish I had asked him what his favorite film was. I should have asked him about a memory he had with my grandmother, who died just a few months after I was born. I should have asked him what it felt like to be a stepfather to eight children. I wish I had asked him why he had never tried to visit us in the United States. But the truth is, I didn't.

On a sunny afternoon, I asked him the same question I asked every day.

"¿Cómo se siente hoy, Abuelo?"

"I can't even drink water. This is no way to live, mija."

He couldn't even drink the mango juices or milkshakes I enjoyed. I never knew how to answer, even when he responded with "good." As if to break the awkward silence, a mango plopped down onto the ground. Before I could grab it and head to the kitchen to peel the skin off, Sleepy beat me to it. The way Sleepy ate the mango, cupping it with his paws and licking with fervor, made my grandfather laugh in a way I hadn't heard since I was a child. The dog scooped mangoes up and licked them dry, ate the tanned red skin, and left the large seed with no gunk on it.

"That dog loves those mangoes," my grandfather said.

"Everybody loves mangoes. Even those damn bats that come visit at night," I said.

"I sure would love a mango," he dared me, looking up to the branches above us, avoiding my gaze.

"Sure, but no salt, remember? Okay, Abuelo?" I said, staring at his dry, almost rusty skin.

"That's fine by me." He shrugged, a sly smile on his face.

I grabbed the long plastic plumbing pipe that served as our mango grabber. The end was large enough to pull the mango from the branch without making it fall and split on the ground.

"Ripe or green?" I asked my grandfather.

"When it's too green, I feel thirsty," he said.

A few minutes later I came back out to the yard with a yellow mango cut up in pieces. We ate with only the sounds of iguanas crawling up the trees above, birds squawking, and Sleepy's licking by our side.

In that moment, I didn't think there was a need to say or ask anything. I was there, sitting next to my grandfather, trying to make the house feel like home. I hoped I'd have more days with him, even if they were in silence.

I have often wondered what made my grandfather land in Milagro of all places. Until my twenties I was aware that he'd run away and built the house and other buildings under his name, even though he had barely received any schooling. I hadn't known why he left. All of his family members, whether maternal or paternal, still resided in the mountainous region in or around Quito. I knew, even though we never spoke about it, that he had run away from the life his parents had wanted for him.

It wasn't until many years later, around my mid-twenties, that I asked for more details about his life. He could have ended up anywhere in Ecuador, and I wanted to know why he decided to put down roots in Milagro. My godmother, who was also my abuelo's niece, told me all she knew about his early life.

Reinaldo was born in Quito in 1935, the last of eight children. His father, Elías, forced all his children to work mining coal on two mountains surrounding Quito: Guagua Monte and Pelagallo. According to my great-great grandfather, there was no need for school but there was a need for work. My great-great grandmother, Victoria, was married to Elías when she was fifteen years old and was known in the neighborhood for feeding homeless children, even though her family could barely afford pencils to send her own children to school. Elías beat her constantly. When she was close to leaving, her mother-in-law would say: "You are a wife now, and that's your husband." So she stayed. When my grandfather was about eight years old, she underwent a devastating operation for her gallbladder from which she did not recover. She had been the warmth away from the soot of coal mining, the retreat from the undulating mountains.

After her death, the children went to live with their maternal grandmother, Rosa. A few years later, Reinaldo realized that he would go up and down mountains with donkeys, carrying coal the rest of his life, if he did what his father wanted. He left and lived with an older brother for some years, working as an apprentice under an esteemed tailor. When he was about sixteen years old, on the Day of the Dead, my grandfather left the highlands of Ecuador without saying goodbye to anybody. When his brother returned from a relative's house, there wasn't even a note waiting for him. It would be more than a decade before his siblings in Quito would see him again.

None of his relatives knew of his whereabouts. When he appeared unannounced back in Quito, he would never divulge how he'd survived the hardships he faced. My grandfather refrained from telling his son, step-children, or grandchildren what he went through during those years. My father once told me he had used newspapers as blankets. Where and for how long, I would never know, but he continued to work as a tailor and eventually began selling products around the country until he landed in Milagro and met my grandmother, Olga. They met when my grandfather was in his early thirties, way past the age a bachelor got married in Ecuador during the 1960s. Olga had been married twice and had eight children, but he didn't care. He was enchanted by her and decided to make her home his home and buy some land that still seemed like a jungle, an area surrounded by mango trees, coconut trees, mosquitoes, iguanas, and dirt. On the day my abuelo turned thirty-six, he had his first and only son, my father, another Reinaldo.

My grandfather left to create his own family, far away from the mountains of the sierra he had known.

On November 28, 2004, my father and abuelo celebrated their birthdays. I still have a photo from that day. In it, my mother, brother, and I are standing behind them in the yard. They are seated with their lips puckered up and blowing candles from a blue cake with the number 69 on it. My abuelo is wearing a sleeveless white shirt—his uniform while sick—and my dad is wearing a gray T-shirt and hat. My forehead looks shiny, and I'm peeking down at my grandfather and smiling. My uncles, my abuelo's adopted children, are surrounding us, and we were all thankful he stole a piece of cake for the special occasion.

A month later, Christmas Eve came along. Mounds of food took up the dining room table. I was dressed in jeans because I hardly ever wore dresses, but all the adults had on their best attire. As we ate, my abuelo looked at his son and said, "Can I have some extra soda?"

Such a trivial question, but I looked at them back and forth as if my grandfather had just asked him for permission to chug some beer.

"Bueno, bueno. Only because it's Christmas," my father said. My grandfather ate more than he was usually allowed. This was the best gift he could have received, but it turned out to be the last meal he would thoroughly enjoy.

On Christmas, when Ecuadorian families lounge around eating leftovers for the entire day, my abuelo didn't feel well enough to leave his bed. The day after, he began complaining about feeling bloated and full. I still thought it was one of his bad days and that he'd soon leave the bed and have enough energy to sit by the hammock. But on the 27th of December, just after the sun had gone down, I heard screams. "¡Algo le pasa a Don Rey!" my mother screamed. The next five minutes felt like they became condensed into ten seconds. I was in my room on the second floor and raced out to the yard. My father ran past the gate, and I heard tires squeal down the street. My mother ran outside too, and I noticed no one had bothered to close the gate. Sleepy was out in the yard, and I caught him just before he started running.

I grabbed his collar, but he began pulling with all his force toward the entrance. No. I couldn't lose them both that night. If I had left everything behind, they both couldn't leave me after mere months. The adrenaline rush of my family screaming and running brought a surge of energy to my veins. I grabbed Sleepy by his paws and dug my nails into his legs until he cried out and stopped pulling. With all my might, I shoved him into his crate. No one was around; I imagined they were all waiting for the doctor on the street. It crossed my mind that the entire neighborhood must have already known something was wrong.

I decided, in those rushing seconds, to check on my abuelo. I opened the door to his room and saw him. Once my eyes settled on him, I knew my dad's race to the doctor was futile. He sat up at the head of the bed wearing a sleeveless T-shirt and a light blue unbuttoned long-sleeve shirt, his silver hair sprouting up like that of a porcupine. His head was contorted to the right, like his body had been in this position, stiff and intact, for days. Abuelo's tongue hung out of his mouth to the right, similar to the characters on cartoon shows I watched when I was a kid. His chest was immobile and his palms were faced upward, at his side, as if he were waiting for someone to grasp them.

I'd made a mistake. I should never have walked in to see him when he was just a body and no longer a body and soul. I couldn't bear to touch him, or even get closer, and I left as if death itself had smacked me across the face. I would never tell my parents, or anyone, that I had seen my abuelo when he had already died.

I ran past the yard but couldn't reach the gate. I felt the roots of the mango trees pull me down to the ground. The energy to get up eluded me. I hadn't realized I was crying, but my shirt was drenched in tears. I felt arms and hands around me. Voices towered over me like gusts of wind that tried to tell me something I could not understand. "Caramelo," I heard someone say. Candy. "Her blood pressure is down," erupted another voice. All they wanted for me was to get up, but the last few months—this new life, this new death—had brought my body splayed out on the floor.

My father came in with the doctor trailing behind him, but I couldn't look at him. Afterward, once I got up, my uncles, my aunts, my mom hovered around me, their limbs like branches holding me up, and all I could hear were my dad's screams.

I didn't have a black dress, so I attended the funeral in a black shirt my parents had bought in the heart of Times Square just six months earlier, a gift before the move. It felt like a decade had passed in those few months. I spent the day of the funeral with my parents or my godmother, Victoria. My parents didn't want my brother to attend the funeral, and he was left at a friend's house to play with children his age.

Victoria and I went across the street from the funeral parlor to have lunch. It seemed surreal how my life had suddenly stopped again. Like an omen, the dish I ordered arrived with two dead flies. My godmother and I, no longer hungry, went back inside to stare at my abuelo's casket.

When it came time to bury him, one of my dad's brothers asked if he wanted to view his father one last time.

"No, I don't look at the dead. Especially not my father. That's not how I want to remember him," he said. I understood but stayed silent. The searing image of my dead grandfather would never leave me.

Men hoisted the black casket and the attendants began to leave, forming a walking caravan of mourners behind the body, stopping traffic along the way. My father, mother, and I were right behind him. A funeral procession was the only time in Milagro when the streets fell silent. The taxis stopped beeping, businesses lowered the volume of their stereos, strangers stood still on the street and made the sign of the cross.

We walked two blocks, and I looked down to make sure I didn't trip over a pothole or mounds of loose pebbles and rocks. We crossed what used to be the town's rail line, and from there I could see the cemetery. There was no field of grass. Hardly any bodies were laid to rest underground. They were stacked in vaults of concrete, three-four-five stacked on one another like sad blocks of Tetris. Before we entered the cemetery, a line of flower vendors stretched across the entire block. Men, women, and their children sold bouquets of roses with intricate banana leaves. Some colors resembled the ripe orange of the mangoes from my house or the bright yellow of bananas. Others were the color of lips, tongues, and blood. The vendors perched themselves outside the cemetery from five a.m.—hoping that relatives would remember their loved ones. They knew there would always be new visitors.

Past the gates we made a left, midway into the cemetery. The air was a mix of fresh roses and bursts of smoke from the candles placed at graves. I could tell whose family members still visited them just by looking at the vaults. Each one was different. Some of them were freshly painted in white with the names, date of birth, and date of death in black. Others had aged, with no one to brush off the dirt that had stuck to the pores of the concrete. The placement of the deceased was in disarray. There was an embellished tomb with various locks from a rich family, a sculpture of the Virgin Mary on top of a grave, and even a recently pillaged casket with blackened blood stains behind a mausoleum. Families who could afford it bought a little gate for their loved one's grave, and in between the gate and vault they would place roses and candles. Visitors who couldn't afford bouquets would often take the ones decorating the graves of strangers.

We reached my grandfather's grave in silence and climbed up a flight of stairs. There was no handrail, and the grave next to it was protected by a chain-link fence with spikes. Once I reached the second floor, there were about twelve graves, stacked atop one another in rows. I looked out above the cemetery and noticed it was bigger than I had imagined. Concrete vaults in stacks—some tall, some short—and not a tree or grass in sight. "Stay close to me," my mom said as she grabbed my hand. There was no wall or railing, and if I stood close to the edge, I could fall on the dead below or onto the people in the procession line beneath us. The men carrying the casket pushed it inside a rectangular vault. Another man, ready with cement, began to seal off the enclosure. My father didn't cry, but my mother couldn't stop the tears. My aunts, uncles, cousins, even men and women I hadn't seen in my life, made a trail by the stairs and onto the floor while a stranger enclosed my abuelo's casket with cement in his final resting place. He would not be buried underground—no earth over him or trees near his grave. I vowed that as long as I was in Milagro, I would visit him with flowers woven in a vivid bouquet and pray to him, requesting his guidance.

Sleepy continued to run away. My father attached a name tag with his telephone number, and strangers would call us and bring him back at all times of the day. One time, a man found Sleepy by the cemetery, and when my uncles, cousins, and father arrived to pick him up, he said, "This dog is loved more than me." A few months later, a taxi ran over Sleepy; he ended up getting stitches, but not even this deterred him from escaping. Robert would sometimes accompany him on his getaways, but he reached the nearby high school and walked right back to our gates, with Sleepy nowhere to be found. One day I was in the bed of a pickup truck when I looked out and said, "I think that's my dog. STOP. That's my dog!"

And it was.

Once, we arrived to our house late at night. The neighborhood had dim streetlights, and it seemed like a dark forest until the yard lights were turned on. I usually walked in dragging my feet, making sure I didn't step in dog poop. But the air had a smell I couldn't pinpoint, rusty like the proteins in dirt, and Sleepy ran and ran and ran in circles, more excited than I had ever seen him. When the lights flooded the yard, my mother and I gasped. The walls of the house were splattered with blood. Sleepy wagged his tail and hovered over a lifeless iguana. His snout was cut, and the water he drank from was stained from all the blood. Usually when the iguanas lost their grip from the mango trees and fell, they scattered right back up the bark and a piece of their tail would fall off as a defense mechanism. Sleepy had always chased them, but I never imagined he'd kill one. The iguana had fought, but it had succumbed to Sleepy's powerful jaws. He sat down and watched us splash our house with hot water. I was on my knees, scrubbing away iguana blood with old towels so it wouldn't soak into the light yellow paint of our house. I took one wall, my mother another, while my father sprayed the house with a hose and my brother petted Sleepy. I couldn't stifle a giggle.

"¿Qué pasa, mija?" my mom asked.

"Nothing. It's just that if someone arrives now, they would probably think we murdered someone and start looking for a body."

"That Sleepy. Es un loco," she said.

But I lied to her. I was laughing because I never thought I'd be a teenager living in the house my father grew up in, washing blood from the walls in my grandfather's absence.

A few months later, Sleepy became a successful runaway. Our new maid had opened the door early one morning and he disappeared. It wasn't until an hour later that my mother woke up and asked her where Sleepy was. He didn't have on his red collar.

"I thought he would come right back," the maid said. But we never saw Sleepy again, and all I could do was pray he'd either found a loving family or a quick death. I wanted to call her a stupid bitch. I wanted my mom to fire her. But my mom reminded me that a woman's well-being was more important than the anger I felt about losing my dog. I wanted the last few months to disappear. I wanted to swing back and forth on the hammock with my grandfather beside me.

CHANGES

When we leave everything in the United States and move back to the country I was born in, I don't think about the little things. Tiny lizards hissing at each other in the moments before sleep envelops me. To leap from my bed and shoo off crickets plastered on my window. Slithering reptiles on my pillow. In just a few months, I sense when an iguana is on the roof, the strides heavy-footed as if it'll fall through and land in my room at any moment. The feral cats' steps feel more like leaps, unless they're mating, and then all that can be heard are shrill screeches. These sounds—needing to live among these animals—won't cross my mind until it's happening. How the constant of a decade's silence in a distant place will prevent a good night of sleep. The buzz of mosquitoes loud enough to keep me up until first light. In the first weeks, their bites ooze on my skin, the scabs itchy long after they have taken what's needed. I learn to breathe under the covers—not allowing a spot of skin as bait.

A pigeon makes a nest on the air conditioner sticking out of my mother's room. She doesn't want to disturb its peace, even when it wakes her up before the jarring alarm. But everything changes when she rouses one day covered in red blotches, and the trail of insects leads to the nest. She enlists the man who isn't afraid of walking on our roof—the one that throws rank mangoes from up high while I hold an old towel with an uncle. Sometimes the mangoes' skin is almost the color of tar, all rotten. The man takes home the just-fallen ripe ones that managed to remain intact. The rest are removed to deter the pulp from cooking under the sun and prevent tiny holes from forming on the tiles so rain doesn't stain our walls. His task on that day is to shoo the pigeon and destroy the nest, but he goes a step further. Our maid makes pigeon broth for dinner. The air conditioners are sealed off at the top so no other creature can make a home, so there's one less thing to interrupt our sleep.

Look at that butterfly, I say, moments after I've put on my pajamas, my mother making her way into my room. *That's not a butterfly,* she says. A moth, perhaps, but her rush tells me that I'm wrong about that assumption too.

A man appears, but I don't remember who—maybe an uncle, or a man from outside our gates. He uses a broom to snatch it from the wall, throws some cloth over it, and carries it to our yard for it to fly into the darkness beyond the trees. My mother holds my hand as we see the distinct wingspread, the pointy corners of its flap, and after I gasp she tells me it's going to be fine, but I don't know if she's talking about them or us. I wonder what it says about me—confusing bats for butterflies.

HEARTBREAK

First, promise yourself you won't fall for anyone in your hometown. Constantly remind yourself never to venture beyond the threshold from "like" to "love." You like Carlos' peculiarities. The way he walks when he wears ankle weights around the sun-scorched town. He won't miss a day at the gym because his body is his home. He can never be still except when his right hand is on your left thigh at the movie theater. You like how you don't have to try to be in sync to music at parties. Your bodies mold together as if they've danced together in a past life.

After a few months, you begin to lose sight of the likes and you start wondering if you crossed the threshold without noticing. You wish there was a word for the midway between like and love.

Oh, but there is, you realize, just not in English.

In Spanish you have *gustar* (to like), *querer* (more than like, less than love, synonym of want), and *amar* (to love). *Querer* is the word you and Carlos begin to use. It's the word couples use when the affection overwhelms them but hasn't overpowered them yet. But you find yourself using those three words to describe him and what he does to you.

You _____ how he uses his hands to explore your body. You _____ it when you say, "no, stop," and he doesn't question it. One day you arrive to his apartment, and his hands have created a drawing on a canvas for you to keep. You ____ that he doesn't have his future figured out yet, but he's sure whatever he'll do will be with his hands, whether it's drawing, painting, or sculpting. His hands will allow him to make a living. A few weeks later, he gifts you a bonsai tree from his family's garden, from earth that belongs to him. You ____ it when he explains how to make sure it doesn't wither and die. You _____ him enough to invite him over for dinner to meet your family.

You hope he won't see how little you speak to your father. You want the evening to zip past so you can both leave. But you _____ the way he converses with each of your parents. The way he reclines his chair back as if he's home. He excuses himself to play a video game with your brother. When he's out of earshot, your father says he walks like a penguin. Buff up top, confident, on his way to reach whatever he wants. It's the first time you laugh at one of your dad's jokes in months. When you leave, hands clasped in a taxi on the way to a party, you laugh when he asks you, "So, do you think they liked me?"

One day you realize there is no need to go between gustar, querer, and amar. The first time he uses the verb "amar," you don't say it back. You ask why.

He intertwines his fingers between yours, gazes into your eyes, and you try to save this moment in your log of memories: "I see you in my mind right before I go to sleep. And I wake up in the mornings and there you are. The first thing I see. That has to be love."

You let the word amar glide from your tongue to his ears. You breathe a sigh of relief that you have decided on the same verb.

Spend every weekend together. Talk about how fathers take their male children to brothels to make them men. Grow furious when he says he would never date a fat person. Tell him he can't take showers while you wait for him in his room because his body tempts you. Tell him you miss walking on streets where there are no dog feces. Explain the difference between your two homes and feel content when he doesn't ask questions, just listens. Ask him if his parents ever fight. Explain that you thought home was a state of being, not a place, but now you just don't know. Dine at the same place you used to dine in with your grandfather. Compare the lack of communication from your fathers. Make a bet on who will end up going to Greece first, even though you've never crossed the Atlantic and he's never been outside of South America.

Bite his lip so hard it almost bleeds. Tell him you're sorry, that your lips lost control, that your body lost control, even though you're fully clothed. Never tell him you're so wet it feels like something is wrong. Stop at the threshold. Place your head on his chest and hold your breath, then ease your sighs until the pulse of your neck is in unison with his heart.

Pretend you're one.

Pretend you don't have to go home.

Pretend that everything will be fine.

Fall asleep and wake as the sun is setting.

LET IT BURN

When the clock strikes twelve, the few cars on the road come to a halt close to the sidewalk until the fires lining every street stop spitting debris. For weeks, Ecuadorians work on their monigotes, or effigies, for this precise moment. These temporary sculptures everyone calls años viejos—"old years"—are molded with plywood, cardboard, and newspaper into anything that represents the past year. Local politicians, Betty Boop, Jon Snow and Daenerys on a dragon, Julian Assange, Michael Jordan and his alien teammates from *Space Jam*. In the hours before the burning, men dress up as widows in borrowed black dresses. Blood-red lipstick smears their cheeks by suppertime. Friends hold a rope from corners of a street to stop traffic. Then the widow seduces the driver, asks for pity, or simply demands ten cents. Even five-cent coins add up to buy explosives and gasoline. One year, an uncle recovers from the verge of death due to prostrate issues and his friends sculpt him, add a woolly wig to mimic his tight black locks, place his doppelganger in a wheelchair, tape a catheter to his crotch, and parade him around a soccer field. When midnight comes, they burn him to ash on the street.

It's Jr.'s turn to choose this year, and once he decides he wants the squirrel from *Ice Age*, we make the año viejo as big as a preteen. Dad buys a pre-made plywood skeleton—the hardest part. Jr. and I crumple up old newspapers to perfect the mold, slather glue, then wait until it's dry so we can paint the eyes and bring life to its face. I mention the monigotes as tall as buildings on the famous street in Guayaquil—art created for destruction—and how people surely start working on them in July. As my father kneels under the fierce December sun, trickles of sweat dampening his tanned forehead, I ask him why we blow up days of hard work.

"Well, why is life hard and then we die?" he says.

We work in silence after that.

A few minutes before the new year, my father begins puncturing the effigy with a knife so my brother and I can force the firecrackers deep inside. Then we all gather our sulfur-stuffed creations by the sidewalk, pyrotechnics drowning out our shouts. At midnight, a man from each home places a monigote in a designated mound. At the end of the bellowing countdown, the fastest man pours gasoline, throws a lit match, and runs away from the sanctioned arson brightening the neighborhood. Mom and Dad only let us watch from behind our gate—afraid a nail might become shrapnel and stab our throats. Standing in my yard, I can hear children wailing because they've grown too attached to their Spider-Man. But everyone watches the burning. Even toddlers. We watch what we've created turn to dust, if only to continue the tradition of letting the past go up in flames.

CRAB FEAST

The wind slapped our faces as we passed sugarcane fields to our right and left. I sat on the bed of the truck with my brother as the warm wind twirled my hair into knots and tempered the humid heat. Half an hour later, we saw a makeshift kiosk that protected some crabs from the equatorial sun. *Ucides occidentalis* live in mangroves, and I'd always wondered how fishermen grab the sneaky suckers. Crabs were tied together in rows stacked on top of each other, eight on top and eight on the bottom or twelve on top and twelve on the bottom. They were strung together with what, from far way, looked like an invisible rope. My brother and I jumped off, and now I'm convinced that on that day, a teenager and a preteen were more of a nuisance than a help.

The man selling the crabs, whose shirt looked two sizes too big and whose skin was so tanned it looked like leather, invited us to look at each row of crabs. The best crabs were found in the outskirts of our town. The locals ripped people off by charging a lot more for crabs, and their front pincers were the same size as their skinny side legs. My uncle drove the truck, and our task was to go back home with the thickest crabs we could find. All the crabs had a blood-red carapace, and some bore a tint of lavender on their extremities. A couple of the meaty pincers had turned gray or white from overuse. They were still alive, as no one would ever sell chilled crab that was already cooked. A dead crab called for an immediate discount—a way for vendors to alleviate their shame. If the front claws were too small, another discount. Tío Pedro always said that we needed to check the crabs tied in the middle. Sometimes the fishermen tricked people by placing the big ones on the outside, to hide the immature baby crabs.

I called out to my uncle and pointed to a row. "Mire Tío, those look pretty big. I call dibs on the one with one eye."

My uncle had done this his whole life, and I was surprised when he agreed. He winked at me, a sign I needed to step back and let him do the talking. Once he picked four sets of a dozen, the next step was to haggle, an Ecuadorian custom I could never perfect. Requesting a few dollars off embarrassed me, but it was a necessity, an expected next step, for all my relatives and friends. My uncle told the vendors he had seen better crabs at the previous two stops—a blatant lie to which my brother and I nodded in agreement. My uncle threatened to leave, another bluff, and once we saw his intentions, we already had our feet on the tires to get into the bed of the truck. It worked, and the vendor took a couple more dollars off the total fee.

We were ready to return with our find, hopeful that all the relatives waiting for us back at our house would approve.

Everyone on the coast of Ecuador eats crab the way New Yorkers love pizza. Although both foods are viewed as more than sustenance, crab is regarded as a near delicacy. A person who cooks crab has to have el toque, the right touch, in order to make cangrejo criollo just right. When I was younger, I assumed eating these crabs was a pastime of all citizens of the world. But once, when I was ten, I made the mistake of ordering them in another country. The waiter put a large crab, the claws the size of an infant's arm, in front of me. It was dry as if it had just been pulled out from under the sun. When I bit into the meat, it lacked all the juicy goo I expected and tasted too much like the depths of the ocean. That crab was a lot bigger than the red ones I ate in my town, and I learned on that day that what matters when it comes to food is the quality, not the quantity. The crabs I've enjoyed devouring, the ones most of the world is sorely missing out on, can only be found from Baja California to Peru.

When we reached our house, my brother and I jumped off the truck and rang the doorbell to announce we had arrived. My uncle took in two sets of crabs while another uncle grabbed the others. We walked into the yard and noticed everyone had finished their tasks. An aunt had put up the hammock between the sturdy mango trees. My mother had just placed the pot and burner outdoors. A cousin had swept the dirt off the floor and placed more than a dozen chairs in the areas shaded from the sun. Another relative made sure a section closed off with mesh screen was clean and had organized the tables into one long row. All we had to do was get the crabs ready.

Tío Pedro carried them to the outhouse sink, and I followed. My brother preferred to sit this part out because he had been nipped too many times. The next step was to cut the rope tying all the crabs together in the outhouse sink. Sometimes it was cut in a way that all of them were set free at once. Imagine a hoard of red tarantulas running for their lives, and if one managed to climb out of the sink and fall to the floor, someone might get their toes nipped. The rope was cut, and on that day we were lucky.

"Bueno, ya sabes cómo agarrarlos." Yes, I knew the drill. He had taught me when I was a visitor in that house on summer vacations. I avoided the side legs and firmly held the front pincers. If your thumb is tied to the palm of your hand, it would be almost impossible to grab a cup. If crabs can't move their front pincers, there is no way they can defend themselves from giants like us. Once I'd secured each hand on the left and right claws, I tilted the crab belly up and put the carapace on the sink. My uncle punctured them with a knife made just for this purpose: right through the abdomen. They became motionless after some seconds. Some Ecuadorians like to boil the crabs alive or place them in the freezer until they stop moving, but my parents dislike making their suffering last. Every time my mom heard someone say this is how they cooked their crabs, she would say: "Ay qué malvados." "How evil."

Tío Pedro's forehead was dotted with sweat. We hardly spoke; our mouths grew silent while we concentrated on the more than forty crabs and listened to music coming from the speakers on the other side of the yard.

We then cleaned the crabs with a brush, scrubbing dirt from the legs and carapace. My mom began preparing the pot. It was so sturdy, I don't remember ever having another one. Even before she placed the crabs inside, she threw in halves of pearl and red onions, sliced tomatoes, a handful of cilantro, and what looked like half a cup of salt. The aroma reached my nostrils and made my mouth water. I still don't know how she cooked such tasty crabs. She had never picked up a cookbook, a measuring cup, or even jotted down recipes. I once asked her how much salt to use for a recipe and she told me she didn't know. "It's the tongue that decides," she said. If she weren't so beautiful—her straight black mane hanging below her shoulders, her petite body bent over the pot—I would have thought she was stirring a witch's brew to cast a spell on us.

The other guests entered unannounced through the gate and sat around the pot with cans of beer in their hands. The children threw around a ball and accidentally kicked the salt container to the floor; some plantain peels ended up on the ground. A mango fell and splatted on my cousin Jonathan's shoulder, and we made sure he was fine before we began to laugh. "Hey, at least it didn't fall on your fat head," another cousin said. Tears of laughter streamed down some of my relatives' faces.

Jonathan picked up the mango and pretended to throw it at whoever had made fun of him, but then peeled the skin off with his fingers and sucked on it before the big meal. Dessert before dinner.

A few times per year, a national law prohibits crab fishing to protect them from extinction, and residents share their anger and longing at work, on social media, and on the street. I am convinced that another reason for Ecuadorians' infatuation with crab is that we could get punished—fined—for eating them during this time. Facebook posts are full of exclamation from relatives who hope not to die before the ban is lifted. Acquaintances who have left Ecuador to reside in other countries plan their trips to visit their homeland according to when it is legal to devour them. Some Ecuadorian residents secretly buy crabs, place them in huge refrigerators, and sell them clandestinely. It's our own version of Prohibition, because people yearn for crabs like liquor. No one ever misses out on a cangrejada. Unless, of course, there has been a death in the family.

It's called a crab feast because it's not something one can cook alone. You need uncles, aunts, loads of spices, beer, wooden mallets, music, and, most of all, patience. A crab feast is an entire-day endeavor where everyone chips in, even if it's just with their mere presence. On that day, I picked out the crabs, killed them, and cleaned them. I had a small role in making everyone's day just a bit tastier.

Right before the water boiled, the beet-colored crustaceans were placed in the pot, ten at a time. I stole a spoonful of the condiment-spiked water to calm my taste buds down when I thought no one was looking. The crabs had to be immersed in the water for just the right amount of time. They can't be in too long, or the fleshy strands will get glued to the shell. If they aren't submerged long enough, the meat will be too raw to eat. That night we had cangrejo criollo, the most popular Ecuadorian crab dish, accompanied with boiled green plantains, spicy beet salad, and white rice. There is also cangrejo chino, or Chinese crab, in which the crabs are marinated in soy sauce and other spices. I once had cangrejo encocado, coconut crab, a tangy mix of flavors that can seduce the taste buds of any human, Ecuadorian or not.

By the time the crabs were ready, everybody was sitting around the row of tables. There was space for twenty people, but somehow about thirty of us fit. The table was covered with old newspapers and the two most important things for nearly every guest: a wooden cutting board and a mallet. I sat down between my cousins, wearing a bleach-stained T-shirt on top of another shirt so the spills and smell, a mix of a mangrove and the ocean, wouldn't linger on my good clothes. The crabs arrived in aluminum trays, and everyone searched for the ones with the biggest pincers. I looked for that one-eyed sucker. There weren't enough mallets for each of us, so everyone waited their turn to break the carapace. The salsa music in the background was drowned by the pounding and the cracking of shells. At the end of the night, everyone's fingers looked wrinkled, like they'd been soaked in a bath.

Some of my relatives ate the big front claws first, but I saved the best part for last. First, I went for the small legs at the sides. Slurping is unavoidable. It's the only way to get the meat out of the little nooks and hinges. I mixed spoonfuls of rice with some of my mom's citrusy radish salad and then sucked on the claws. The tangy onion taste of the salad meshed well with the salty meat. An aunt liked to tell everyone who would listen that she remembered the first time I ate crabs when I was a one-year-old. I'd dipped my tiny hands into the crab juice as I sat in a high chair and licked my wrists to the top of my fingertips.

I bashed open the thick pincer. When I'd hammered it perfectly, so that nothing stuck to the inner shell, I interrupted the conversation around me to demand the recognition I deserved. I showed my prize to everyone around the table. Those who were not engrossed in the meat of their own crabs raised their first or hollered their approval in Spanish. Tío Pedro winked at me. A perfect shattering of the shell.

BETWEEN
BORDERS

CHAIN MIGRATION

My mother doesn't remember the change of seasons, her mother's smile, or the home in Stamford, Connecticut, where she spent the first years of her life. When she's three and her older sister is five, they become orphans due to fate and a man's choice. Their mother is diagnosed with aplastic anemia and dies just a few months later, and their widower father refuses to be the sole guardian of two girls. There is a third child, one born with the privilege of a penis. The father sends the two girls more than three thousand miles away, to the country he originally migrated from, and reserves his fatherly duties for the boy who can stay with him in the United States.

The girls are sent to Milagro, Ecuador, a coastal town about an hour away from the hub of Guayaquil. Despite its name, the town lacks miracles, though it makes up for it in sugar and pineapples. A river, in which the town's kids swim, weaves through its center. The sugar mill's tower rises above most of the edifices and cloaks the air with a hint of molasses, while slivers of ash from the factory fall on clothes hung out to dry across the town, like a volcano emitting a persistent spew of smoke. In the 1970s most of the streets are still dirt. The few concrete ones bear the onslaught of the rainy season for four months, and by the time April arrives and schools open, the streets are battered with holes the width and depth of pots made for gumbo. With only two main streets, it takes just a few minutes to enter from the east and continue onto the outskirts of the town, where only sugarcane fields and rice fields mark the landscape.

Dictionary.com:
"An **anchor baby** is a child who was purposefully brought while in the womb to the United States by a foreigner so that they would receive US citizenship upon their birth. It is widely considered to be an offensive term to immigrants, especially Asian-Americans."

The sisters first live with their maternal grandmother. About a year later, Tía Yolanda, one of their father's eight siblings, visits the girls. She finds them both on the sidewalk. They have long unkempt hair, and even though they are two years apart, they are both the same height. Their skinny bodies are tanned from the equatorial sun, and the oldest is a few shades darker than her sister. Their shirts are worn through with holes, and they are sweaty, with old dirt on their necks, new dirt on their fingers, and Tía Yolanda initially mistakes the lice crawling on their faces for moles. She claims the girls, taking them to the house she shares with her mother and brother.

That first night, she heats up water and bathes them. She pours lice shampoo on their small heads, caresses their scalp, and makes sure none of it seeps into their eyes. Tía Yolanda, a teacher who prayed for children of her own, is granted the children of her brother by Diosito. The girls sleep in a separate bed in her room. She can finally be a mother, kiss her quasi-children goodnight, and for years the girls don't understand how good they have it.

Tía Yolanda is plump but petite, with black hair that almost reaches her shoulders. She never leaves home without lipstick or mascara, which makes her small eyes pop. Men look back to take in her beauty, especially on the monthly bus ride with the girls to the US Consulate in Guayaquil. When the gringo officials see the girls, their guardian is handed a Social Security check for each of them, which is financial help from the government due to their mother's death. It is more money than what Tía Yolanda earns in six months at her teaching job. She then takes the girls to their favorite restaurant, where they eat juicy meat, moros con lenteja, and leave with protruded bellies. The girls always wear matching socks, clean under-wear, and dresses with no holes. They are enrolled in their small town's most expensive school and attend an English academy on the weekends. "It's for you to understand basic English once you move back to the United States after high school," she tells them. Tía Yolanda promises the girls that no matter what happens, they will attend a bilingual high school in Guayaquil. The girls will have to wake up at five a.m., make new friends, and start homework on the bus back home, but it will all be worth it. Every year, during the months of school vacation, the girls go with Tía Yolanda to the United States for a few weeks, a treat paid for by Tía Alba, who lives in Stamford, Connecticut.

In November 1986, President Reagan signed the Immigration Reform and Control Act. Reagan's joint statement declared, "Very soon many of these men and women will be able to step into the sunlight and, ultimately, if they choose, they may become Americans." In 1990 the cost for a US citizenship application was $90. By September 2020, the cost had increased to $640. As of October 3, 2020, the new fee was $1,170.

The girls only see their father during annual trips to the United States. I can't imagine how it must have felt to know that your father is still alive, thousands of miles away, unwilling to reach out. He doesn't write, he doesn't call, and he doesn't send money. But they are children, and children love their father. They hug him when they arrive at his home in Connecticut, call him Papi, and are polite to his new Argentinean wife. They also visit Tía Alba, who visits the girls every year in Ecuador, sends them new clothes, and continuously asks Tía Yolanda whether they need anything.

According to the article "New Media and the 'Anchor Baby' Boom," published in the Journal of Computer-Mediated Communication *in 2011, the term* **anchor child** *"describes a young immigrant who will petition relatives in other countries to become permanent residents or citizens of the United States."*

When my mother is twelve, Tía Yolanda falls ill with pancreatic cancer, and Tía Alba does everything in her power to take her to see a doctor in the United States. But before Tía Yolanda can leave, she undergoes emergency surgery in Guayaquil. She will never regain her strength to stand up and teach. The girls hear her crying out in pain for weeks. At times Tía Yolanda stifles her moans so the girls can sleep. Her bosom, once wide and full enough to allow a toddler to comfortably sleep in, begins to disappear. Her waist shrinks until her clothes cover her like bedsheets.

The night she dies, the girls cry themselves to sleep: the oldest one because a second mother is gone, and the youngest because, while it's not the first mother who dies, it's the one she will remember. Their future paths are again wholly altered by death. An uncle takes them in, but uses the Social Security checks to support his love of whiskey. The girls never go to school in Guayaquil, and they don't learn English. They leave the private high school and enroll in the overcrowded public one. The uncle's number-one priority for the next few years is to make sure the worst fate doesn't befall them: premarital pregnancy. He only lets the girls out of his sight to go to school, and then they must head straight home after the last school bell rings. But my mother meets my dad when she's in high school, and she sneaks out to see him. When school is closed for the holidays, the girls lie to their uncle and say they indeed have class to experience some semblance of freedom.

At seventeen, my mother becomes pregnant with me. Somehow my mother, father, and their friends keep it a secret from their guardians. If they hadn't, she would have been forced to drop out during her senior year. People think a pregnant girl in class is contagious and will lead to more children out of wedlock. In their high school graduation photo, my father and mother are standing side by side, along with my paternal grandfather. Their expressions don't look mischievous at all, but their ability to keep a secret is one of the reasons they're smiling. In a few weeks, when she is four months pregnant and she knows no one will be able to take away her high school diploma, my mom and dad confess. My mother's uncles and aunts call her father, and it's only then that he decides his presence is warranted.

Excerpt from Chapter Three of the US Citizenship and Immigration Services Policy Manual: United States Citizens at Birth (INA 301 and 309):

"A child born outside of the United States and its outlying possessions acquires citizenship at birth if:

- The child was born before noon (Eastern Standard Time) May 24, 1934;
- The child's father is an alien;
- The child's mother was a US citizen at the time of the child's birth; and
- The child's US citizen mother resided in the United States prior to the child's birth."

My parents remember that the day after I'm born, my maternal grandfather arrives in Milagro. He stands in the doorway of my mother's room, demanding she promptly get dressed in white and walk down the aisle. The second worst thing after premarital pregnancy is no marriage after a birth. My father promises he'll take care of my mom and me, but a wedding is out of the question. They're still teens, and no one forces my dad to do anything he hasn't decided to do himself. Mom and Dad leave with me wrapped in a blanket and they move in with my paternal grandparents—but without a promise to wed. The man who abandoned my mother was left reeling in shame for what she did to the family name. Decades later, my mother's father will ask me to call him Uncle instead of Grandpa, so I refuse to call him either.

No one outside my immediate family knows that when I'm born, my mother is given a document that says *Certificate of Birth Abroad of a Citizen of the United States of America* with my name on it. My father learns his girlfriend doesn't have an Ecuadorian passport just a few months before I'm born. For years, no one knows that my mother is, on paper, actually a gringa. No one knows because she doesn't speak English and because the trips to the United States had stopped years before.

In 2008 a "birther" controversy erupted during Barack Obama's candidacy for president of the United States. It began when opponents alleged he was born outside of the country. On August 6, 2012, Donald Trump tweeted: "An 'extremely credible source' has called my office and told me that @BarackObama's birth certificate is a fraud."

In July 2008 Fred Hollander filed a lawsuit against John McCain and the Republican National Committee in order to disqualify the Republican candidate from the US presidency. The suit alleged that McCain couldn't become president because he was born in Coco Solo, Panama, on August 29, 1936. At the time, the Panama Canal was under US control.

I was born in 1989, and by the early 1990s, my abuelo was one of the wealthiest people in Milagro. After my father graduates from high school, Abuelo gives him the money and the space to start his own business. In a few years, though, he is on the verge of closing his business for the second time. He refuses another loan. Instead, at twenty-four years old, he decides to go to the United States and start over. His father is adamant that he stay and tries to convince him that the perils of immigration aren't for him. But his pride doesn't allow him to stay in Ecuador.

My parents, now married for several years, arrive at the US Embassy. They've consulted lawyers, filled out paperwork, obtained bank statements—but they're still worried. Green cards are rarely granted, so they're scared he might have to wait a few years or go back to the embassy in a few months. The workers don't even peek at the paperwork. Instead they ask who I am. My father grabs me by my armpits and raises me up to the gringos. In that moment I become their anchor to the United States. I look like my father, and they tell them that's all they need. He has a green card within a month and leaves to start a new life in Connecticut before we can join him.

In 2020 the Trump administration announced a travel ban on Kyrgyzstan, Myanmar (Burma), Nigeria, Eritrea, Tanzania, and Sudan. These countries were added to a previous list of countries with travel restrictions, which initially included Iraq, Syria, Iran, Libya, Somalia, and Yemen. Rep. Sheila Jackson Lee, D-Texas, called the new travel ban "pure discrimination and racism."

I'm five when we join my father in Connecticut. My mom has papeles but no command of English and only finds work cleaning houses. In 1996, on a day toward the end of spring, late to one of my mother's appointments, we board the first train heading south. Mr. Cutacelli will be at the Greenwich train station to pick us up to clean his home while I'm left in a room to play with toys that aren't mine. My mother doesn't like to venture to an unknown location if she's alone. When she needs to take a bus or train, her knowledge of English evaporates, and she enters into a rush of panic over what the unknown could bring. She fears a train will end up in New Jersey or Florida, far from the comfort of all that she knows. On the train, she suddenly notices that it isn't making any stops. There should be five stops between South Norwalk and Greenwich, but the train proceeds at a high speed, and by the time we approach the platform, my mother is holding back tears. She spots and waves at Mr. Cutacelli, the house owner who promised to pick us up. The train doesn't stop, and my mother looks around for a face that might know Spanish to find out where we are heading.

On Saturday, September 21, 2019, Cristina Riofrio sat a table with friends in a McDonald's in Georgia. A man at a nearby table overheard her speaking Spanish and ordered her to "shut up" and "speak English." She filmed the encounter then posted it on Twitter and wrote, "In America, I can speak FUCKING Spanish if I want to." Cristina was born in California to Ecuadorian parents. I think, That could have been me. *Not only are my parents Ecuadorian, my mother's maiden name is Riofrio.*

Within a week, the man who hassled Cristina was fired by his employer, the Chatham County Sheriff's Office.

My mother finds a conductor aboard the train and explains as best she can. Her hand, holding mine, is wet with worry.

"Grenich. No stop? Stop in Grenich?" my mother says.

"Oh, you got the express train, honey. Next time take the local. LOO-CAAAL."

He stretches out the vowels as if this will prevent any future mix-ups, as if my mother knows what these words mean. The man has some stubble over his lips, and I can't see his hair under the navy-blue conductor's hat. His shirt is a lighter blue, the color of a cloudless day. "Don't worry, I'll tell you which train to get on once we stop so you can head back to Greenwich. Sit down, okay?" The other passengers have books or newspapers open, some are wearing T-shirts or light sweaters and they glare at us, others have worried eyes, but they are all bound by silence.

"Mami, are we okay?" I ask. If she cries, I'll panic. But I don't see any tears, and she tells me there is nothing to worry about it. I cling onto her like I always have. I'm five and I have never had a nanny. She is everything to me. I make sure I'm touching her hand or arm, and I feel like the weight of our worry is like a heavy anchor that will cause the train to halt.

I have never seen the end of train tracks before. In my mind the tracks circled around the world in a never-ending path to take people to their destinations. The terminus is not what I imagine. The track is covered with trash, from coffee cups to old newspapers and receipts accidentally flung from people's pockets. We are the only ones who cross the track to the other side; everyone else on the train makes their way past the railings, through a gloomy tunnel to wherever they need to be.

We thank the conductor and head back toward Connecticut. Cell phones are not common yet, and my mother doesn't have a beeper; we can only hope Mr. Cutacelli is still at the station and not eager to fire her. When we arrive at the Greenwich stop, about an hour and a half after my mother waved to him from the express train, he knows exactly what happened to us and is ready to take us to clean his home.

In 2018, on a televised show called Axios *on HBO, President Donald Trump said: "We're the only country in the world where a person comes in and has a baby, and the baby is essentially a citizen of the United States . . . with all of those benefits. . . . It's ridiculous. It's ridiculous. And it has to end."*

What I don't know on that day, when my mother utters "I'm sorry" too many times on the train platform, is that she is not an immigrant to this country. What I don't know, even to this day, is who the anchor child is. Is it me or is it my mother? Maybe it's both of us. What I don't know on that day is that my mother was born just a few miles from where Mr. Cutacelli stood, beaming with an expression of pity reserved for newcomers who don't know the difference between the express or the local train.

CAT WHISTLES AND WOLF CALLS

Twelve Years Old. *The First Cat Call.*

A few months after 9/11 my family moved from a neighborhood with tattered chain-link fences to a house with a manicured lawn. It was a mere ten minutes from the apartment in Norwalk, Connecticut, that had been my home for most of my life. I knew it was a better neighborhood because no barrier separated the front yard from the street. My mom announced that she would finally have her own garden. I was helping her on a spring morning until she finally convinced me to take off a pair of oversized gloves and leave her with the quasi-gardening. I went inside but left the door open to the front yard.

Some minutes later a voice erupted: "Hey sexy, those pants look good on you." I knew it wasn't my father, not because he would never say that but because he only spoke in Spanish. I thought I wouldn't hear the voice again. Then a scream: "Yo bitch, I'm talking to you." I ran out to the porch and called out to my mom. I stared at a white man hunching over the passenger side seat of his car parked in front of our yard, while she walked in without looking back.

I had dreams for weeks. In them, the man forced his way into our home while shouting the word "bitch" again, grabbed my mother, and demanded an answer to his accolade.

My mother never learned how to garden.

Thirteen Years Old. *Boys Will Be Boys.*

A teenage boy or a young adult—all I know is he still has no hair above his upper lip—plasters a sign against the backseat car window. "Show me your tits." The van they're in is the color of old burgundy. The driver darts his eyes from I-95 to the woman in front of me, the one in the passenger seat, waiting to see if she will lift up her shirt. The boy's two friends surround him, and they are all inaudibly pleading "please."

The woman, Carolina, laughs and tells her husband to look at these dumb kids. They continue to beg her, and they don't stop even when her burly husband eyes them. "Him or me?" she asks them. "You, you, of course, you," they mouth. She pretends to lift up her shirt as their eyes stop blinking. Instead, right before she reaches her bra, she lowers it and points to her husband. "Him, right?" They don't say no, just shake their heads side to side in frustration. We switch lanes, and the almost-man lets the paper fall from the window.

Sixteen Years Old. *Indecent Exposure.*

Instead of hailing a one-dollar taxi that could take us anywhere in my hometown of Milagro, Ecuador, my cousin and I decide to walk. We continuously shake our heads at the men in taxis and illegal taxicabs that beep at us. Some of the beeps are actually programmed with recordings of wolf whistles. Every time they pass by and I catch a glimpse of a man in a yellow cab, I picture him at a car shop, asking for his car to be waxed, to make sure they check the brakes, and not to forget to add an automated wolf whistle. That way he won't have to pucker his lips together and waste a breath. With a tap of a button, all the women his car passes by can hear the sound of lust.

We avoid the people on bicycles and walk carefully as the railing of the bridge peculiarly only reaches below our waists. Suddenly we hear a *tsss tsss* sound. We would never deliberately connect eye to eye to a catcaller, but the sound is coming from the strait of dirt and grass almost below the bridge, to our right, a sliver of earth between the buildings and the river. How he got down there bewilders me, but not as much as seeing his half-erect penis. He has just pulled his pants down to his ankles, pressing his heels on them to get them completely off. And now, as he stares at us in our tank tops and jeans, he strokes himself up and down with angry enthusiasm.

I quickly focus my eyes on the road and upcoming cars, and my cousin can't do anything but laugh nervously. I hope that he won't get into the dirt-brown river. It's filled with dog carcasses, discarded beer cans that can easily cut flesh, and the residuals from the local garbage dump. But it would be of no use to say anything. This naked man is fraught with uncombed curls and a torso with accumulated shades of dirt. A word from me may be an invitation to leap toward us or to prompt him to share his fantasies. Instead, we walk faster, and to this day I wonder if he waded into the water, got pulled by the current, and ended the day with brackish water in his lungs. I'm sure he didn't. I'm sure he waited to *tsss tsss* some other girls behind us.

Seventeen Years Old. *The Wolf.*

The three of us are walking in our hometown about a block away from our destination. Our bodies are teetering on womanhood, but our minds are still confounded by teenage tendencies. We walk arm in arm—giddy, happy, worried about the crushes we'll see later tonight. We're almost done crossing the intersection, five steps away from the sidewalk, when a man riding a rusted turquoise bicycle stops in between us and our goal.

"I'd fuck all three of you, but all three of your pussies stink."

I wait for one of my friends to say something, but neither of us can take our eyes off his graying beard and ingrained wrinkles.

Men have told us they want to be the fart in between our butt cheeks. They have told me that they could but won't touch me now because I'm not ripe yet, as if I were a tender mango being primed for their bite. This insult in the guise of a catcall has caught us off guard. This stranger wants us to ponder his words, question our bodies, and make us believe we're filthy. His brown eyes are scathing. They bounce from each of us to see which brave girl will cuss him out. It's anger he wants. This is the sentence he's used to draw ire out of girls: foul words or wads of spit.

"Keep on going, old man."

My words come out quick and lenient, more like directions instead of the fury bubbling inside me. He won't have the pleasure of seeing his words hurt me. The man accepts my command and quickly pedals away without another word. We get to the sidewalk, our arms no longer linked, wondering in silence if our pussies indeed stink.

Eighteen Years Old. *Vile Whispers.*

"Treacherous butterfly." The lyrics emit from the speakers of the blue bus. A song in Spanish about a butterfly, a woman, flying from petal to petal, mouth to mouth. I am in the aisle, holding onto a seat, carefully placing my hand not to touch the man's head sitting in front of me. Bodies are scrunched tight together, and the stale, tangy, and dense types of sweat mesh into a sheet of dampness. The equatorial sun is as fierce as any other day.

A man places himself behind me but does not touch me. He shuffles to a position where his mouth is inches from my ear. I feel the whisper disturb my skin, triggering goose bumps, as he sings the lyrics to me. I ignore him, but unable to move my feet, I tilt my neck as far from him as I can. The man in the seat looks up at me and winces but stays silent. I refuse to look at their eyes, and stare out to the green Ecuadorian landscape passing before me. "You have a butterfly," he says during the guitar riff. He is referring to the monarch butterfly tattooed on my back. I forget it's there sometimes, but I can always count on strange men to remind me. The man sings to me, even when the song is over, repeating until I get off the bus that I'm a treacherous butterfly.

Twenty Years Old. *Worldwide Prey.*

We are on the outskirts of Madrid, almost noon, at a train stop near the city of Getafe. My bag makes me stick out like a tourist, and we walk a few blocks to my friend's apartment. A man appears behind us and says something, but his accent is so thick that I can't process the words. Carla grabs my shoulder and says, "Run." My feet begin to fly on the sidewalk from a surge of adrenaline, hands flailing, bag weighing me down, my chest heaving from an unprepared sprint. He continues to jog toward us, just a few feet away now, determined to touch us. We stop on the opposite street, looking back to check if he's near us. All we can see is the hair on his head and bright green of his jacket, walking back toward the almost-empty train station.

I ask Carla what he said. "Let me touch that sweet ass." We vow not to come back via train later that night.

Twenty-seven Years Old. *Just Another Day in the City.*

I go to New York City in search of delectation: Broadway shows, book readings, and museum exhibits that beckon me. I plan the days from morning to night, squeeze events until they almost overlap like how the ladies on the subway squeeze into their black leggings, tight enough that the white-and-red stripes of their panties seep through. I enjoy the city more by myself. Alone, I can linger in the subway platform as men pound on pan steel drums and visitors, travelers, and tourists film them and shake their heads in unison. Alone, I can spend the hours I want surveying art at whichever museum I choose, being as idle or as swift as I like in between the Renaissance and Cubism paintings. Alone, I do what I want when I want.

In New York City, though, the men in the streets constantly remind you that you are never alone, that they will not be ignored. As I head to the nearest subway on a bright morning, just a mere block from where the train from Connecticut has just left me, two men inch closer to me. At arm's length, with the surety that I can hear them, one utters: "Oooh, look at this bitch." "Oh yes, who does this bitch think she is looking like that?" says the other man. It's early winter, and I have on a black coat, black leggings, black everything. I don't know what I look like, if I'm a mark of longing or disgust. If my panties show through my black leggings. I'm sure their faces will provide an answer, but I don't dare look back. I keep on walking to the subway station, brewing with anger that I didn't say anything. I wish they had appeared toward my departure, not my arrival, so the rest of the day would not have been tainted by their words.

Twenty-eight Years Old. *Trust No Man.*

It's past eleven p.m., and my day in New York City is ending. I'm in the Harlem 125th station printing my train ticket for the ride to Connecticut. Tonight, there are just a few people in the lobby. I walk away with my ticket in hand as a man calls out to me in Spanish. He points to where I have just left and asks if this is where he can buy a ticket. "*Sí*," I say, and start to walk away.

"Wait, can you buy me a ticket?" he says.

The man assumes I will say yes again, and he pulls out his wallet. But in my gut, fingertips, and chest, I feel it. My body tells me not to get close. That maybe it's just a facade and he'll say something that will make my blood fester. Or maybe he'll touch me. I don't say no. Instead, I tell him, even though he has a credit card stretched out toward me, that the kiosk has the Español function. "You can do it," I say. The man lets his hand fall to the side in anger. His eyes tell me I've betrayed him, like I've broken the solidarity of our shared language. I never see him again.

I hope my eyes explained what I couldn't.

Stranger, many men have demeaned and insulted me during my twenty-eight years on earth. I cannot trust you. If you are a kind man who truly seeks help, I'm sorry, and I wish you knew what I've gone through and why I won't risk edging my body toward yours. If not, fuck you.

I would rather ignore a stranger, process the guilt, and shed a tear on my way home because I refused to help an immigrant, a Spanish-speaker, a man in need. But I'm resolute in my decision. I will do the same tomorrow or five years from now. It's why I don't lock eyes with strangers on public transportation. It's the reason I cross the street to avoid a group of men.

It's how I protect myself.

THE FIRST TEST

I was a bilingual in a room full of monolinguals where they made requests to hear the sounds of unintelligible sentences in English that piqued their fancy. I loathed entertaining their boring requests. If they told me to say tortuga, I said "turtle"; if they told me to say casa, I would say "house"; if they told me to say cucaracha, I lied to them and said the German word krakerlaken; if they told me to say hijo de puta, I would say "son of a bitch." And then I'd say, but that's the usual phrase for the term, what you'll see on the captions in movies, but it's not all true, because sometimes the soul of words, even the word puta, is lost. Puta means "whore"; "bitch" means perra. But no one says "son of a whore" in English. All of this I could explain, but when they asked me to say whatever I wanted, whatever came to my head, just to hear the peculiar sound of my accent—say whatever the mold of my tongue felt like flinging to their ready ears— my throat would grow jittery, my eyes would zigzag, my mind would flip the catalog of weird sentences that I could say: "The house has a pig farm in the attic." "I'm not a motherfucking parrot." "I could be insulting your mother, grandmother, and your entire ancestral line and you would never know." "You're not even really damn interested in what I have to say, just my accent." "Do you ever wonder what languages we would have, what customs we would practice, if America was never colonized?"

These were the requests of my teenage classmates in Ecuador, in the country I was born in but where I had not grown up, sitting in a class where I was learning Spanish, my first language that had been eclipsed by English when I moved for a decade to the United States. When they were bored, and this was often, the requests came. One day there was a request from my teacher. She wanted to know the translation of the song title "Sk8er Boi" by Avril Lavigne. Why was there an ocho in the first word? "Skochoer Boi, Skochoer Boi, Skochoer Boi, what does that mean?" she asked. The students waited for my answer, their expectant stares waiting for a coherent explanation. But how to explain that the title only works in English? If I said that, they would have slapped their tongues to the roof of their mouths, rolled their eyes, and believed I was a fake. I wanted to say: That title is lost on non-English speakers, and this is just how you have to live your life, not knowing why there's an ocho in the title. Sorry, your loss. Just like people all over the world have had to come up with in a foreign language what Michael Jackson meant when he said, "Beat it, just beat it." But I didn't want the profesora to think I was a pompous brat, because she already thought I was a brat. I stood up and walked to the white board.

You have to read the number in English: 8 = "eight," not ocho. But even before that, you have to know that "Sk8er" is actually a different way to write "skater." The sound, the play on words makes *ate* sound like *eight*. I said all of this to a group of students sitting at their desks, tilting their heads, writing down notes as if this was to be on an upcoming test.

Eight = ate = skate = skater = sk8er.

No, "sk8er" isn't a real word. No, you won't find it in the dictionary, I said. "Boi," neither, because it's a purposeful misspelling of the word "boy." The writer was just playing with the sounds and not imagining that a bilingual Spanish speaker would have to get into phonetics to explain.

OK, the profesora said; now translate the entire song.

Sure, Miss, can you let me sit down and go through the lyrics?

Bueno; this will be your homework, she said.

I went home and translated the lyrics line by line, hitting a roadblock when I came to the word "punk." What was the equivalent to a skater punk when there wasn't a skate park in this entire town? How could I bring the essence of what a gringo punk meant to the ecuatorianos in my classroom? And how could I explain to them that it was not the same as an old man finding a kid egging his house the day before Halloween and yelling "you little punk"? I ravished my brain completing the most difficult homework I had ever had, but felt a surge of pleasure each time I solved a term. How could I translate "rock each other's world" without making it sound sexual and getting reprimanded by the profesora? Or what term could I use without inserting the word "rock," piedra, in Spanish? I hated the teacher each time a five-letter word halted me for more time than I could bear. But it was on that day, after I reached the last line—sobre una chica que solías conocer—that I knew what I wanted to do for the rest of my life.

Revive words on a page, conduct a dissection of their phonetic energy, feast on their syntactical order, and create a passage into another language where words would be built to invoke the same feeling to the reader or listener. I didn't know on that day if I would always be successful, but I knew I had to try, and, most of all, I knew I would never spend so much brain power on a translation without getting paid for the mental energy that Avril Lavigne had drained out of me. I don't remember the teacher's name, but that homework sent me on a path that would define my life, a step beyond being bilingual, and into the painstaking work of what it meant to become a translator.

TEETH FRAGMENTS

After Christine Byl

1. A father and son were once in my mouth at the
    same time with a hammer and chisel. My mouth
    is too small for my teeth, and their task was to
    make space. There was no pain, but the hits scolded
    my eardrums. I caught a glimpse of the shattered
    tooth when it was over, after one of them said that
    my wisdom teeth had more curves than my body.
    Their laughs like the ache of a molar when it's dead;
    they hadn't known I had famished myself for years.
    When I got home, my jaw grew to the size of a
    bruised heart, the red and blue veins slithering to
    my ear. The cavity would become infected, but I
    never went back.

2. Underwater, touching sea-soaked sand, sharks
    trapeze around Christine Zenato, urging to be
    petted like puppies. They linger around her palms as
    if she's singing to them through touch. One day she
    reaches inside a mouth as a row of daggers surround

her arm. Zenato retrieves a fisherman's hook. *To relieve their pain*, she says. She knows when the moment has arrived for her to insert and pull out the sharp edge. No bite, no teeth on human flesh. After more than three hundred removals, the sharks still ravage around in the moment of the pull, but they come back to lay their heads on her as a gesture of gratitude.

3. Where are your baby teeth? Did she keep them? Your mother. Or did she throw that part of you away as soon as it left your body?

4. If our teeth were bones, they would heal themselves after chipping. The decay, whether one cavity or sawed-off molars from sugar, can't be healed. It can be halted to show a more aesthetically-pleasing facade. A serial killer—with more than ten murders and ten rapes—ignored his teeth to an extent that a composite police sketch saved some space just to show the rot of his gums. When caught, Richard Ramirez spent more than two decades on death row, where dentists worked on perfecting the remaining teeth inside his mouth with taxpayer money.

5. To teethe. I marvel at the *e* at the end. How this one letter converts a noun into a verb, how it evokes the fussiness of a child, the desire to bite and alleviate torn gums. When I want to translate this verb into Spanish, the need to use too many words in a plump sentence leaves me disappointed.

6. My mouth has been numbed by anesthesia more times than I can recall. As a teenager, metal chained my teeth twice. My teeth rebel—the gums too dainty and weak. The dentists tell me they don't know why my gums change from the color of fallopian tubes in some parts to the dark of puddle water in others. *Do what you need to do*, I say. When too much time passes, I miss the anesthesia injection penetrating the roof of my mouth, as if longing for the preceding moment of the pull squeeze drill waver strike when I already know feeling will be absent.

7. I hadn't heard about the tooth fairy until there was no way I could believe in it. Not because I didn't receive cash from my parents. I did—whenever I failed to swallow a tooth and felt a gap in my gums the size of my wants. But in my first language it was a mouse's duty to remove the tooth from under my pillow and leave the cash. I would imagine the switch of tooth and bills with its snout, making sure I didn't wake. No fairy, no wings, no stories made in my image. But, like in all recounted myths, the tooth serves as payment to another being as an ode to who you once were.

FIRST COMES THE EGG

When my father comes home and a cicada's mating call cuts through the silence, he lunges rocks toward the trees, wherever it's loudest. It's bad luck, he says. I watch my mother bathe in a tub with Pepsi—a witch's order. It's to rid her of a spell another woman cast on her, she says. One day, a dead mouse is on our concrete front yard. Neither the neck nor extremities show any evidence of life being purged from it by force. Dad is doubtful that a bird of prey freed it midair. It seems *placed* there. A natural death is bad luck or someone's up to some brujería, my dad says. He disposes of it like he's doing a séance, saying prayers to spirits and making sure something made of wood or metal is between him and the rodent at all times. All the babies I meet wear red. A bright bracelet or ripped-up cerise paper on their foreheads with spit. It's for good luck, to ward off the evil eye, to stop a wicked spell in its tracks, everyone says.

When I am a child, a curandera takes an uncooked egg and glides it over my skin when I look wan. The shell feels like faience on my skin—cool silk, gentle enough to shatter. For me, it's a massage, but my parents consider it a diagnosis of brujería, bad luck, the evil eye, or a sickness that justifies a visit to a doctor. When the curandera breaks the egg and places the albumen and yolk in a clear glass of water, I stare at the veins of her hands that spread like roots to her ashen arms. The loose fibers swell from the yolk, and the proteins make mazelike webs and tell her all she needs to know. Each time it's done, I wonder what effect the egg's energy would have on me if I ate it. But I don't eat it; I just stare, looking for the answer that is clear to her but a riddle to me.

When I am a woman, a cousin and I talk about our parents' ways. We reminiscence on the times eggs are caressed around our necks, the slight pressure of an oval at the bridge of our noses, not knowing this is also the same substance as coarse seashells. She tells me how the ritual cures her child. I look at her, incredulous, waiting for her to confess she's joking. Instead, she mentions how years ago her son was always nauseated. His skin has red splotches every few weeks, and he becomes too thin. She worries, and her mom announces that if doctors can't solve the enigma, surely an egg will. The grandmother takes it upon herself to be a curandera. She begins to do to him what has been done to me, my cousin, my father, my mother, and those who came before us while saying out loud the Padre Nuestro. I wonder: *How can she read the raw egg in a glass without training?* But the egg is never cracked, my cousin explains. Before her mother is finished, the baby bursts in blemishes, his skin prodded on like a swarm of mosquitoes just enjoyed a sucking feast. The boy cries out, his chest begins to tighten, and they rush to the hospital. Days later a physician provides a list of allergies that could induce anaphylactic shock. Eggs are forbidden.

I share this anecdote at reunions, with fellow Ecuadorians, with people from other cultures who tell me their parents own rituals. Burning just the tip of a newspaper in an ear to relieve pain. Burying tiny sculptures of santos in the front yard to ward off evil spirits. Limpias from a shaman when hope is finite. I no longer live where I grew up—there's no neighborhood curandera to visit me. But sometimes, when no one is around, I purse an egg to my cheek, follow the path of my lips, before cracking it, wondering what the chalazae is trying to tell me. Then, when the egg is cooked to a soft boil, I place it in my mouth and feel like I'm eating a piece of myself. All the while acknowledging how much we're beholden to the ways of our ancestors.

THE DIAMOND OF MY EYE

If my eyes spoke, they would scream.

They pounce out like the eyes of a coquí. The sclera is too abundant, while the iris and pupil shine like a small lone brown island in a sea of white. My enemies yelled out FROG when they saw me in grade school. I hated the eyes the universe had granted me. When I was a kid, I hoped they would recede into my face, unable to imagine how my eyes would become the frailest part of my body.

My eyes transformed from a self-esteem issue to a medical issue in my teens. When my family and I moved from Connecticut to Ecuador in 2004, they began to bother me. There were a few months when it looked like the oil glands of my left eye were producing dandruff. Eventually my eye doctor had to numb my lower eyelid to remove a discharge that had accumulated on the edge. I lie on the chair, thinking, *This could be worse. At least I have nothing pulling my eyelids open like in A Clockwork Orange.* I stared up at the ceiling while the doctor rubbed, thankful that I didn't feel anything. The only reason I knew what was happening was by snooping with the corner of my eye. The rhythmic motions of the doctor's hand moved side to side, taking all the poison out. White goo oozed out of the tiny pores. She showed me everything that had accumulated on her utensils, as if she had filed away a candle with a minuscule cheese grater.

The issues didn't end there. I developed sties every few months. The word for "sty" in Spanish is urzuelo, and I think this is the most appropriate-sounding word to describe the pain. "Sty" is too quick, just one syllable. The word in Spanish, though, consists of three syllables: ur-zue-lo. The letter *z* gives the word its oomph. *Z* is one of the least-used letters in the Spanish and English languages. It's right there, in the middle, creating a sizzling sound. It sizzles, it burns, it sears. This is how an urzuelo feels like.

"Oh mija, everyone gets urzuelos," my dad would say. They were as dangerous as cold sores to my parents. According to my dad, all I had to do to get rid of one was to place a spoon in the freezer for ten minutes and then place it on my eye. I had my eye spoon ready to go in the freezer at all times as a precaution. The constant issues made me limit contact lens use. Part of the problem stemmed from the small city I lived in off the coast of Ecuador, which was battered in dust and filled with exhaust smoke from buses made in the '90s. I couldn't bear wearing contact lenses for extended periods of time. I felt my eyelids sprout tears and fight to push the dirty specs of dust out of my eyes whenever I ventured beyond the walls of my house.

My brother and I have eyes that swell, unlike my parents. Unlike anyone in our family. Our bus ride from my hometown to school was an hour to and from our house, so we often napped. One of the girls would place a sweater over my brother's face and mention that she just couldn't take it. "He's the only person I've ever seen that sleeps with his eyes open," she once said. When my brother and I sleep, our eyelids serve as curtains with insufficient cloth. You can see the irises flow slowly around like a dead goldfish floating on the surface of water. Our eyes scare teenage girls, and when I tried to nap on the bus, I forced my eyelids to touch and hope that they never opened while I slept.

After the move to Ecuador, I spiraled into a deep depression. I lost my appetite, and at 5' 2" I weighed less than a hundred pounds. When I stared into the mirror, it looked like my eyes had taken over my face. Someone once said, maybe a friend or an uncle or a bully, *All you are is eyes and bones*. But what bothered me the most were my eyelids. I wasn't sure if it was because of my weight or because one eye had indeed seeped further back into its socket, but the creases of each of my top eyelids met at a different place. I was convinced it deformed my face, making my eyes uneven.

As the months and years passed and I regained my appetite and fought the depression, any intent to gain weight was futile. I ended up in a clinic or hospital every six months. Once, after eating some tainted crabmeat, I was checked into a hospital and lost ten pounds in one week. When I got home, new pink stretch marks spread on my inner thighs, scars that would forever remind me of my stomach's inability to get used to the bacteria in Ecuadorian food. I remained a body of corners, while my eyes remained the only plump and curved parts. People no longer yelled out FROG, not like how childhood bullies used to do, but their comments and jokes were microaggressions that continued to chip away at me.

One night in my late teens, I was at a dance club. An acquaintance, a man I had spoken with a few times, talked to everyone—except me—with his eyes forced open. When he spoke to me or our eyes met, he would release them to their natural position. As he chatted to everyone around me with his eyes open wide with a look of surprise, I pretended not to notice. I ignored the girls trying to hide their chuckles within the drums of the music, but I knew it was a nod to me and how I appeared to everyone around me. In a country where slim waists and thick busts and thighs were coveted, I looked like puberty hadn't hit me yet. All around me I heard people discuss the 90-60-90 measurements for a perfect female body. Ninety centimeters around the bust, sixty centimeters around the waist, and ninety again around the butt—impossible numbers for my own frame.

I didn't cry until I got home. I wouldn't let them witness how the mockery affected me. The face in the mirror didn't feel like the person I felt when I walked to the bus stop, when I put on high heels, or when I sat down to read a book. It felt like a mask. I thought about all the girls I knew from high school. They got nose jobs. Doctors reshaped their chins. A friend even got her lopsided ears fixed. But my eyes? And my slim skeletal figure that contributed to it? It seemed like there was nothing I could do about it. So I stopped looking in the mirror unless necessary. I would dust some bronzer on my cheeks and put on some lipstick, but I avoided looking at my eyes for years.

I moved back to the United States in 2012, when I was twenty-two, and within the first month I gained more than ten pounds. I still ate my mother's Ecuadorian food, which was all we could afford to eat, but I no longer felt sick every few weeks or stashed Pepto in the fridge. Today I joke that my palate loves Ecuadorian food but my stomach is indeed an insipid gringa. Once I moved, the maladies disappeared, and meat began to settle on the contours of my bony face. I went from a size double 0 to a size 2 in a matter of weeks, and I could gauge the difference by how my shoulders transformed from sticks to full-fledged arms. My jeans wouldn't close. My dimples were more profound with the extra plumpness covering my face. My eyelids were still uneven, but I was no longer *just* a pair of eyes. I finally didn't have to force myself to look at the face I was given in the mirror. I also said goodbye to the glasses that covered my face, wearing them less and less.

For a couple of years, I continued to suffer from occasional sties, but nothing too extreme. They popped up and went away after a few weeks or so. Then, as time went on, I began to feel slight changes. If I drove for an hour with just a hint of sunlight, my eyes would begin to cry. I would feel water flow out past my cheeks and soak my neck. It felt like someone had blown specs of pepper into my face as I drove. I wished for green lights to become red so I could shut my eyes until the waterworks stopped. If I had endured the piercing equatorial sun, I couldn't understand how some sunlight in Connecticut would make my eyes cry at random moments.

As I arrived to my job one morning, my right eye and eyelid began to throb like a heart. I entered the bathroom to inspect my eye. And there it was. A tiny white dot on my iris. I was lucky that on that day I was able to get a walk-in appointment with my eye doctor. I was diagnosed with an infection that, left untreated, could have led to a worse outcome, like a scratched cornea or blindness. Blindness? The word made me realize how serious the issue could have become. I convinced myself that I would have never allowed it to reach the extent of losing my eyesight. But the way I treated my eyes had to change. I could no longer wear biweekly contact lenses. I had to switch to daily ones. And I had to limit the time I wore them. But it was a relief, an infection caught right on time. I did what I was told, convinced that the worst was behind me.

A few days before Thanksgiving 2017, my left eyelid became thick and enveloped in red. I had suffered from sties at least once a year during my life, but this *felt* different. I had a small red ball on my upper eyelid, but my entire eye stung as if it had been taken out and placed over a bonfire. The following day I woke up and looked in the mirror; my top and bottom left eyelid had become the size of a mandarin, like blood needed to be drained from it. My eye was blemished in red. I took a picture and sent it to my boss, who insisted that I stay home for as long as I needed. *This is it*, I thought; *this is how I will stay forever*. I had this overwhelming feeling that my eye would remain like that until I died, and I panicked. If before I had cried about mismatching eyelids, I scrunched up into a fetal position and bawled. Just when I had reached a point where I was fine with my face, my body, my eyes, something came out to put me back in the place I had fought to leave. Whether I was in Ecuador or the United States, I couldn't escape the eyes I had been given.

Every time I cried, the fleshier and more tender my left eye became. I cried even more when I learned I couldn't get an appointment with my ophthalmologist. Under my company's new insurance plan, I had to have authorization from my primary care doctor, and she couldn't see me until after Thanksgiving. My eye went unchecked for days, shrinking throughout the day, but going back to the juicy size every morning when I woke up. Almost two weeks passed before I could see my ophthalmologist.

After I'd endured twenty-eight years of eye issues, a new doctor finally articulated why I had been suffering throughout most of my life. Blepharitis: inflammation of the eyelids—a result of oil glands that close and become inflamed. The yearly sties, the infections, the constant tears from too much light, the need to have screens at the lowest level of brightness, the gooey swelling, the morning pain just to open my eyes, the irregular rheum that lined my eyes. There was a reason for my weak eyes, and it actually had a name. I was devastated when the doctor explained that blepharitis is an incurable chronic illness. It can be controlled, but it will never go away, and flare-ups may happen if I'm not careful. No more mascara, eyeliner, and eye makeup. I cringed.

"How did I get this? Is there something I could have done to prevent it?" I asked.

"Well, um, you know how some people just never have acne, some have mild acne, and some have terrible acne?" he said. Dr. Fox looked like he was in his late thirties, with thinning black hair and a rehearsed smile. I pictured a photo of him smiling with perfect teeth on a bus advertisement. He just looked the part. I didn't say yes or no to his question.

"O . . . kay."

"Well, some people just have blepharitis and some people don't. Sometimes people have it their whole lives and don't even know because it's so mild. But, you know, by looking at your history here, it seems like you're prone to infections." He smiled with all my paperwork in his hands.

I guessed it was just my body that was both the perpetrator of pain and the sufferer.

"How long do flare-ups last?"

"Everyone is different," he said. "Weeks, maybe months." I sensed that he wanted me out of there quickly. I had my diagnosis, and now it was time to leave. In that moment, I vowed that if I saw his photo plastered somewhere I would deface it. He had finally found a diagnosis to my eye woes, but he was being a dick about it.

"I'll prescribe you a gel to put into your eye and something to take the swelling down. The best thing to do, and this is going to sound weird, but take a sock—clean, of course—fill it with rice, put it in the microwave for thirty seconds, and just place it over your eye. This takes a lot of patience, but make sure you do it several times a day."

I don't know which solution seemed more like a prank, my dad and his freezing spoon or my doctor with a sock full of rice.

I had to bury my sadness within my lungs, within the cavities inside my body, instead of sprouting them through my eyes. Every time I cried, my thick eye really did deform my face. Instead of simmering down, it would remain inflamed, a stark contrast to my right eye. I couldn't suppress how ugly I felt, because now it was definite that how I felt was how I looked. It was a painful sickness, and one that is not invisible. My blundered eye was the first thing someone saw when they looked at me. It didn't help that while people stared, there was a stinging and throbbing reminding me why. Apart from looking and feeling ugly, I would wake up with what felt like sand between my eyes. For months I felt like my eyes parted in the morning like wax pulling hair from skin.

I googled everything about blepharitis after the diagnosis. I even gave the red bump on my upper eyelid the name Claude, and I have photographic evidence of his evolution saved in a folder on my phone. While I was able to find studies and eye doctor sites, I could hardly find any blogs or websites by people who had been diagnosed with it. Eventually I found a couple blepharitis support groups on Facebook with about eight thousand members. My flare-up lasted from November until February of the following year, and through the Facebook group I learned that there are indeed people who suffer longer than I did. Some, and it had never occurred to me until I saw photos, have flare-ups in both eyes. If I'm in a public place and searching through the group, I make sure no one can see the gory photos. People post pictures of their swollen, watery eyes, with pinkish veils for eyelids and missing eyelashes. Most of the posts ask the perpetual question: What helped you?

There are threads about manuka honey, tea tree oil, specialized shampoos, diets, lash cleaners, at-home concoctions, and antibiotics to stop the unbearable throbbing. At first I thought the manuka honey was placed over the eyes, but then I read posts by people who eat a spoonful of manuka honey every day and this keeps the flare-ups at bay. Members discuss which tea tree oil shampoo has stopped symptoms. They specify which cleanser is too rough on their eyelids. And when someone needs more than medical suggestions, they are able to receive emotional support too. When I looked up the word "suicide" in the search bar for one group, there were at least fifty posts mentioning the word, and more responses from the community urging posters to reconsider, to seek help, or just to write that they had once thought about ending their lives too.

We all post about doctors that don't take us seriously and tell us there is nothing more to do than place a wet cloth on top of our eyes.

These are just a few examples of the posts:

Eye doctors. Tell me something I don't know. #frustrated
Wow, I sure got in trouble for calling my eye doc. I guess I

had too many questions. He sure wanted to get off the phone quickly. Especially when I told him I was in a support group and people were all complaining about their eye doctors. LOL

Tks God (and my mother) I've studied the English language and had the great idea to search the word "blepharitis" on FB. Because I did not find any important information about this condition in Portuguese, not even with the 4 docs I've been to.

My eye doctor tried to help but ran out of options, and my primary care doctor thinks I'm complaining about an "inconvenience."

We are all in front of screens, aware of the pain the screens might trigger, but we find solace in empathizing and connecting with each other.

I sometimes joke that the Facebook group has helped me more than any doctor has. It's not too far-fetched. Only we know how it feels to have this illness. All of us have experienced the feeling of wanting to hide when people look at our faces and wince. Our eyes feel terrible and look terrible. But everyone is willing to share how they got better. And through exhaustive Google searching and the groups, I have had few flare-ups since 2017.

My brother still has eyelids that don't close completely when he goes to sleep. He's never had a flare-up like me, but his eyes are constantly red. He blames allergies, and to this day I insist that he see an eye doctor. Without the diagnosis, I would never have identified certain aspects of my life that I needed to change.

I only wear makeup if I'm invited to a wedding. I limit wearing contact lenses to one day per month. I use cotton swabs to clean my eyes daily. Every week, I wipe my eyes in a special eye cleanser. Tea tree and anti-dandruff shampoos are terrible for my hair, but I use the shampoo on my eyebrows, slowly letting it fall on my eyelids on the days I wake up with what feel like tiny specs of rocks in my eyes. Whenever there is a slight hint of pain when I wake up, I place heated pads on my eyelids. I don't rub my eyes. I try not to touch them. I wear sunglasses on sunny days to prevent my eyes from tearing up. I can't drive without stopping every few hours to give my eyes a breather. If I begin to believe that I've been cured and start slipping on my cleansing regimen, my eyes immediately remind me with crusty rheum that I will have to maintain this careful daily upkeep forever.

For me, one of the side effects of this illness is envy. Whenever I hear the cliché about how the eyes are the mirror of the soul, I want to show people photos of my flare-ups. At least eight thousand Facebook friends would agree that our eyes do not reflect our souls. I envy those who tell me they wear the same pair of contact lenses for two months. I have to remind my family members during reunions that I'm not crying from emotion; I just can't control when they water. At times I feel frustrated at the amount of time I have to dedicate to my eye upkeep and then leave the house without a smidge of makeup around them. Sadness enveloped me when I threw away my eighty-color eye shadow palette. I wish I could place some mascara on my lash line, but it's like clogging plumbing with coal.

I often look at the picture of the worst flare-up of my life. It reminds me of a few things. It reminds me that I spent my entire adolescence thinking my eyes were deformed and that, as I grew older, I was shown what deformity and pain really looked like. To this day, even when someone can look at me and not notice a thing, I wake up feeling like my eyes produce crusty sand. The photo is also there to remind me that one day in the future, my eyes will flare up and scare me and everyone around me. I have overcome them in the past, and I need to trust that I will be able to do so when the time comes. I have come to accept that, although I have some control, I will never be able to cure this chronic illness.

It has often felt like doctors have had to chisel away at the muck surrounding my eyes to keep them healthy. I've also had to dig to the depths of my body and self-esteem to consider my eyes of worth. I used to detest my eyes, to repeat the word "hate," "hate," "hate" when describing them. But now I just say my eyes are bothering me. The uneven creases bother me. The gunk bothers me. The way it sometimes feels like my eyes aren't circles but pointy diamonds bothers me. Each day, I wake up and look in the mirror and feel thankful when a flare-up hasn't come back. Yes, it was only when my eyes' innate purpose was threatened that I began to fully appreciate their beauty. I have never loved my eyes, and I probably never will, but the difference today is that I want them.

THE TRANSLATOR

My brother places his scrawny right hand over his stomach and uses his weight to tilt the chair backward. Only the rear legs are touching the ground.

"What a good orgasm," he utters with a smile.

I look to my mother at the head of the dinner table. Her eyes are scrunched up, fighting the laughter that will spray the soup from her mouth onto her children's plates. She gulps and begins to laugh.

"Did you tell him that's what an orgasm is?" I ask her.

"He's only ten. I'd have to explain sex if I explained what an orgasm is."

The pleasure my brother received from the food has vanished. The chair is flat on the ground, and he's slouched in embarrassment, staring at his plate.

Mom, Mami, Madre, Ma, Mother. I think of how to start my sentence to explain the severity of the situation. I want to call her by her first name: Shirley. But we're Ecuadorians, and we don't call our parents by their first names. Just like English speakers never name their sons Jesus. An unwritten rule.

"Madre, if he asks, he's old enough to know." School has taken care of the word "sex," so I explain the word "orgasm."

"You know how good it felt, like right now, when you were eating? Sex feels good too. Well, sex or masturbation. There comes a moment it's so good that your body wants it to be over. It explodes and you feel it everywhere. That's an orgasm. Just don't say 'What a good orgasm' ever again, okay?"

My mother says, "Thank you, mija."

Years later, when my brother is nineteen and I'm twenty-five, the three of us are watching the film *Atonement*. The second time the word "cunt" has been uttered, my mother asks:

"¿Qué es cunt?" "What is cunt?"

My brother looks at me to make it clear he will not take up the role of dictionary on this day. My eyes wander in circular motions, searching for the correct answer, the right words, a tone of voice that won't make my Spanish-speaking mother feel dumb.

"Mami, the dictionary definition is 'vagina.' The character says he wants to taste her cunt. This is not a negative context. But it's usually an insult, like 'asshole' or 'carade-verga.' The word is really harsh in the United States but not as strong in Europe."

She says, "Gracias, mija." I wonder if she's asked others the definitions of foul words.

"Ma, whenever you don't know a word, you can ask me or my brother. Google helps if we're not around," I say. She nods, and I think of my mother's innocence, oblivious to words that wound.

I arrive at my mother's apartment, and she says we need to speak in private. She has only said this a few times to me in my life, and I prepare to be chastised. She smacks the door of her room and whispers to me, "Mija, the condom broke. I'm forty-five. I can't get pregnant again."

I sigh and place my hands on her shoulders.

"I can't be a sister any more than you can be a mother again. Take your purse and a bottle of water. Follow me."

The nearest pharmacy is five minutes away. We head to the aisle—white pregnancy tests, diapers, yeast infection creams, panty liners, genital soap. I can't find it. I go to the front to ask the man at the counter.

"Do you have the day-after pill?"

"Yes," he says and begins rummaging out of our view. My mother is behind me. She's wearing high heels that she clings to during the weekends; her arms lack flab; glossy hair falls buoyantly beyond her shoulders. People gasp when they overhear me calling her "Mother." She looks like a naive college student, like my sister.

The man shows us a clear plastic box and pulls it apart to give us the wrapped pill. She signs the keypad in the rush of a woman determined to stop the spermatozoids from implanting her waiting egg. When we get in the car, she doesn't put on her seatbelt.

"Thank you, mija. I don't even know how I would have asked for this," she says, gulping down the tiny pill before I can turn the key in the ignition.

HAIR IN THREE FORMS

My black hair can only be tamed when it's burned. An iron to my head, not too close to my scalp, but enough to feel the scorching steam. I make a straight line with a finger between my ears, put the top half in clips secured near my scalp, cup the strands, and start the process. My hair closest to my neck is the unruliest, the most knotted, like the crisscross of cables weighing down a telephone pole. Close to my forehead the hair makes waves. In a ponytail the hairs stand up at attention like pine trees poking out in a dark forest. I have a mestiza's hair. The hereditary mix of the indigenous and the colonizers of my ancestral line.

I speak Spanish and English in the countries I live back and forth in for most of my life: Ecuador and the United States. In Spanish we have three words for hair: pelo, vello, and cabello. My parents teach me that pelo simply means "hair," all hair, from the fur on a baby penguin to the hair in your nose. Vello is the hair on your arms, torso, stomach. The hair that rises to attention when alerted by goose bumps. Cabello is the hair on top of your head, the one the world first sees.

My pelo and vello can't be tamed by heat. When I hit puberty, the onslaught of my period isn't as cruel as the pelo that arrives to take up space on my body. When I go to a pool, a girl asks why my legs have so many red dots all over them. "Are they mosquito bites?" she says. I lie and say yes. I'd rather say this than explain that my pelos are so thick they thrust out of me like razors. My hair hurts my skin. When I shave, my legs bloom in red flares. If I stop, the irritation leaves but my legs become draped in thick black hairs. I have to choose between red blotches or black strands. I want to be hairless. I want the brown of my skin to remain uninterrupted by internal forces.

At the pool I look at girl's and women's stomachs. I don't care if their abdominal muscles are tight or if their skin sags. I want to see if they have the same circular trail of dark vellos surrounding their belly buttons; none of them do, just the men. The hair on my stomach grows like a field of dark wheat, except they are not cultivated in straight lines. At the base of my belly button the vellos point north, south, east, and west. The short hairs above it twirl to my right. They are there, dark. I loathe them more than any other hairs on my body. If I shave them, my stomach will be home to prickly pointers that will announce themselves in force, just like the ones on my legs. I despise these hairs more than the lone hairs that appear around my areolas. At least these can be hidden at the pool. They can be plucked enough that they disappear for weeks at a time. But at the pool I can't hide the pelos on my arms, legs, and stomach.

I shave my armpits for two years, and when I'm fifteen I notice that they are tainted. The skin looks like it's been blotched with a gleaming coat of coal. This skin here is darker than the color around my shoulders and the point where my breasts meet my side. I envy the girls that raise their hand and no bristles of pelo are seen and their axillar skin is the same color as the rest of their body. A friend tells me that waxing decreases the black shadow. I get a wax, and prickles of blood appear in the crevices of my armpit, but I feel it lightening with pain at every tug. The waxer tells me that this method can also make the red on my legs disappear. I accept I can only acquire hairless beauty through pain.

Once I'm in high school, my cabello becomes an issue. My parents call me leona, lioness, because my hair grows like a lion's. To the side or up, as if in shock. My strands don't point downward or flow in straight lines like the blonde girls at my school. I go to a salon, and a woman tells me she can take away the bulk. She shows me a special scissor. One edge has a line of teeth and the other is straight like any other scissor. She begins to cut, and threads begin to fall until it seems like a small dog is snuggled on the floor. She cuts my hair, blow-dries it, and straightens my unruly cabello. When she is done in exasperation and drenched in sweat, she announces that cutting my hair is like cutting five people's hair. She doesn't know I can never forget how my hair makes others feel, but all I do is smile and give her an extra tip. My cabello tires fingers, hands, arms, like they are taming an unruly lion.

My mother tells me she's heard of a treatment that will make my hair normal. To make it look less like the erratic frizz I was born with and more like her hair, which hardly requires a comb when she wakes up in the morning. The treatment is called keratin, and it will leave my hair soft, straight, easy to weave my hands through. She pays two hundred dollars, and I spend half a day at the salon. Beige gunk is straddled on my hair, left to seep, and then the chemical is burned with an iron. I hold a wet towel over my eyes and nose. Google searches have indicated the chemicals may be carcinogens. I hold my breath as steam emits from my hair. A man comes in to pick up a package, screams at the owner to open up the window because the place smells like acid.

My hair can only be tamed when it's burned. But the chemicals only last for six months; forever would be too much to ask. People tell me my face has changed, they tell me it suits me. They ask me what I did. I release my scalp from the tug of my ponytail. My arms don't hurt when I blow-dry my hair. For the first time I feel like I have cabello on my head and not pelo. This is what it feels to be born lucky, to be born with the right commingling of genes.

I follow this ritual of cleansing my body from unwanted hair for years, until my cabello has been emaciated by the heat. The desire to stop burning and stripping hair from my body grows as slowly as the hairs beneath the knuckles of my hands. When I'm in my late twenties, controlling the cabello, pelo, and vellos becomes more of a nuisance than the hairs themselves.

One day I decide to donate my foot-long hair to a child with cancer. I cut it until the hair is barely three inches above my scalp. It's a pixie cut, and I don't tell anyone about my plans so I'm not persuaded to do otherwise. When my boyfriend sees me, his eyes flash in shock and he asks me why. I'm tired, I tell him. I'm tired of blow-drying my hair until my arms are heavy. I'm tired of spending money to eliminate a temporary nuisance. I'm tired of having strangers rip my pubis, of having to hold back tears with every tug. I'm tired of looking down at the vellos of my stomach in shame when I shower. I'm tired of hating my hair. I'm too tired to continue working toward hairless beauty. What's the point? It always announces it will be back in full force in its natural form.

The trajectory has drifted from hate but is far from love. It's in the intersection between like and acceptance. I can't stop what is logical, essential, inherent. The process of protein, follicle, and root thrives on the landscape of my epidermis. I allow the vellos on my body to grow just like a cat accepts its fur until it needs to prune it with its tongue. I reach less for the hot wax, iron, and razor. Some months, I don't reach for them at all. I watch the pelos grow under my armpit, on my stomach, on the creases of my knee. I am unlearning to see this as ugly and animalistic. I allow my hair to bloom because I am alive.

LAST TOUCH

Our lives parallel each other. We're both dragged from somewhere else—he from Quito. His mom is a former beauty queen; mine just a known beauty without the official crown. This connects us, and now so does the loss of control over our bodies. Too young to fend for ourselves and run away, or, as we both don't want to admit, too scared to leave our privileges, getting fed by others, going to a private school. We're bound to our high school, the scratch of our uniforms, our parents' need to fulfill promises to themselves and not us. We find other things that connect us. Our fluency in English, listening to music no one else does, the sphere-shaped beauty mark where our left thumbs end and the rest of our hands begin. Maybe he notices or I do; the thing is, one of us is looking at the other's hands, maybe imagining what it feels like to trace them over each other's body, looking for what will make it gasp. One of us says, *The same shape, the same place, just a different color*. Then he places his hand on top of mine, knuckles on knuckles, and I almost melt, as if I were paper and he fire, and I am left wanting him to interlace his fingers with mine. We share a sign on the map of our bodies. This is as much as we'll touch before he graduates, when he tells me he'll leave this godforsaken town to join a rock band. *You don't need to explain, I feel the need to leave too*, I want to say. But I'm jealous and tell him *me harás falta*, not using the word "miss," but "lack," because in Spanish I can explain better what his departure means to me. He leaves, both of us wanting the place where we meet to become a memory.

It's the last day of the year, maybe a year or two after I graduate from high school, and I'm outside a club in my town. Or maybe I've just convinced myself of this, and it was just another day where I forget about leaving by doing what I always do—dancing. Still in the same place, still without a way to leave that doesn't require begging. I feel lonely, the way I know the people who surround me will only be around if I have something spiked with tonic water in my cup. I remember waiting, either waiting to get in or waiting for someone to come out, just waiting. Then I hear the bellow of my name. And for a moment there is silence while everyone stares at Miguel walking toward me. And I'm surprised by my instinct, running toward him as if our mouths had once already met. I anticipate a hug, but first I get a twirl, the spin dizzying as much as the smell of his skin. There's only a kiss on the cheek, and a hug that lasts too long when I take in a tinge of cologne seeped in what I believe is marijuana. He almost looks the same, although more rugged, his arms full biceps, white skin, dark brown eyes. He's not dressed for the club, but as if he were coming to perform with his band—carefree, loose jeans, black high-top sneakers. We talk for too long; he says he'll always be back to visit his mom, and I'm surprised by the way my body exhales around him. I tell him the truth, how I feel suffocated, trying to find my way back, say *tú sabes cómo es*, still not feeling like this is where I should be. He tells me about the Galapagos, and I imagine whales breaching in unison. When we say goodbye—my friends staring, whispering, a hint of surprise in their body language—I know our lives will always intersect in this place.

The next time we meet is years later, not a coincidence but a plan. I'm still in our town, but I can count the weeks before my flight. My house is empty of people except for me and a dog that is not mine but is entrusted to my care. I first go to his parents' house because he's just visiting, always visiting, between touring in Europe and other countries. We have lunch then listen to music, watch Die Antwoord videos, listen to cadences I've never heard. I tell him to come over tonight, and he does. I don't remember the first kiss, more the first touch, when his hands grip tight around my waist and pull me to him. We explore each room as a heavy rainstorm pummels the roof. Our fingers braid with each other's as he's in me, and I think of the ways that delaying is tact. How I knew years ago that our skin didn't just parallel but that it could deliver us to each other. We teach our hands to move, to search for the marks our clothes hid for too long. When we're done, I trace the hard line of his clavicle with my fingers. I expect sleep, but he and I are wide awake, looking at the curves we took in during the frenzy. *¿Alguna vez has meditado?* he says. I confess that I can't quell my thoughts, leave my mind blank, but that I'll try. We sit on the bed, our legs crossed, and he grabs each of my hands with both of his to make the tips of my fingers come together like a tulip still closed, the petals still feeding before the flourish. He asks me to close my eyes, and we unite our voices in a hum, making my breath follow his, the rain gone but the drips falling, the windows still wet, letting our lungs fill with the wait of the other.

THE NORTHERN HEMISPHERE

THE GARBAGE
COLLECTOR'S DAUGHTER

My father and I share the same shade of maple syrup skin. Hardly anyone has said I look like my mother, but if you saw Papi and I walking side by side, you would know we're related. We have round faces, the same plump cheeks and skinny nose. While my big eyes can only be mine, the bone structure that surrounds them is a copy of his face. Our similarities go beyond our physical attributes. We're both stubborn. When we believe in something, nothing can budge our opinions. We hold grudges. If you get on our shit list, maybe we'll remove you in the afterlife. I forgive, but I don't forget. He does neither. These similar personality traits have been the reason conversations between us result in shouting matches and hurt feelings. Now that I'm thirty, I know which topics are safe or when to simply walk away. What has always been a safe topic, and what continues to bring us together, is garbage.

My father has worked for private garbage companies since his early twenties. It's just him and his truck. He's the driver and the thrower. For most of his life, he has picked up garbage in the wealthiest towns of Connecticut. One of them is the town of Greenwich, which is the home of hedge fund managers and presidents of Fortune 500 companies. In 2017 it became the home of at least ten billionaires. It's not merely a town of the well-off, it's a secluded town of only the 1 percent. From decades of being a garbage collector's daughter, I've learned how easily they throw away things that a middle- or working-class person never would.

When I was younger, at least once every week my father would arrive home with a find. There was once a Saks Fifth Avenue cashmere sweater with the tag still attached. A pink Nikon camera. An unopened box of colorful markers. A television. But the finds that spurred conversations between us were the best. Every few months he would find a watch that didn't tell time, and he would challenge himself to fix it. We would sit at the dining room table and he would use a minute screwdriver to twist and poke. After he removed the outer case, he'd ask me to pass him a different screwdriver and keep on working. This was the moment I usually began asking him about his day or discussed the task before him.

"Look, these gringos have so much money, they don't realize this is fixable," he said.

"Well, they can afford a new pair, Papi."

"I should sell stuff on eBay."

"Or you can give them to me," I said and winked.

If he didn't arrive throughout the week with a find, he came home with a story. They ranged from the weird, silly, and laughter-inducing. He told me all the stories in Spanish. My dad could make the mundane seem interesting. He acted out the encounter with a racoon that hissed at him. "I hissed right back at him. Louder, enough that he got scared and jumped out of the garbage can and ran away from *me*. I don't want to get rabies," he said. He told me never to tell anyone about the heavy white garbage bag that split open once he threw it in his truck and dildos of all shapes, sizes, and colors popped up. "Pero es que hubo un montón. There were so many of them I wondered what made her throw them all out at once. Just weird." I remember the story he told me about 9/11. He kept picking up garbage on that day until a woman in a multimillion-dollar home urged him inside. "I had on my work clothes. Smelly. Dirt on my boots. But she insisted I sit and watch the news with her. We were two Americans, just an old lady and me, watching history on the nine o'clock morning news." He's described the smile of the little kid that waves at him every Thursday morning, waiting for his favorite garbage man to honk the horn.

Garbage is an easy topic to discuss with my father because all others cause tension. It's neutral territory, intertwined in gifts and projects. Anything else can spur a screaming match—especially when I was younger. What I've often thought is an innocuous comment or small talk would result in my father somehow picking a side, a mound that would evolve into a hill—a hill on which he would die and manage to take hostages in the process. Now that I'm an adult and my father is about to turn fifty, I know how to avoid the implosion of our communication.

When I asked him back in 2016 why he wouldn't vote in the Democratic primary election, he said: "Why would I vote for Hillary twice? I know she's going to win the Democratic nomination."

"No one knows that for sure."

"Yes, we do. Talk to anybody. It's the most logical step. Bush, Clinton, Bush, Obama, now it's time for another Clinton."

"But that's not how it works."

"Mamita, come on, you're a smart woman . . ."

The "mamita" came out with an emphasis on the vowels, the annoyance too obvious. When I heard mamita, I knew we were close to raising our voices. So I just ignored whatever he said next.

"Whatever, Dad. Just vote in the main election then."

A day or two after coronavirus appeared all over the news, my dad sent a meme that alluded that the illness had started because a Chinese person ate a cat. It was similar to the ones that popped up on my Twitter and Facebook feeds before fear and obituaries took over, and I imagined he knew what I would think before he sent it to our group chat with other family members.

I messaged back: "That's racist."

He sent back a line of the simultaneously laughing and crying emoji.

"It's a joke, not racist. Besides, I only do it because it bothers you so much," he said to me later that day.

"That's almost as bad as being racist, Dad."

"You take everything too seriously."

I don't recall much about the last topic that caused us to screamed at each other. I've made sure it was a few years ago, but I remember stopping by his apartment to say hello after work. He was wearing a long-sleeved black shirt, and swaths of lotion seeped into his red-stained cheeks. As usual, he was telling me a story. His hands flailed in the air while he took his time with the details, some of which he'd already shared with me earlier that week. I said, "Pa, you already told me this part. Can you get to the part I don't know?"

"Never mind." His two-word response was swift, and he lowered his hands and began to look at his phone.

"What do you mean 'never mind'? JUST TELL ME WHAT HAPPENED. THE PART I DON'T KNOW."

"Ya, no. I'm not telling you."

He didn't speak to me for twenty-four hours, but the following day he pretended like nothing had happened. There is a list of topics I know not to discuss in depth with him. Politics. Any type of shooting that appears on the news. The best taco places in our town. The prodding into Aaron Hernandez's sexuality in that recent Netflix special. (I think they spent too much time on it; he believes it was necessary.) The past. The future.

It's difficult to talk to others about my father's occupation. The first time I told a group of people what my dad did for a living, I was in the fifth grade, about ten minutes from my school on a trip to Cove Island Park in Stamford, Connecticut. The other fifth graders and I told one another what our dads did for a living. Teacher, construction worker, a girl who said her dad had to read a lot of books and that's all she knew, store manager, and more. I said garbage man. No one made fun of me or said "ewww." But they said "oh" like they were really trying to say, "Oh, you poor little brown girl." Then I showed them the atomic purple Game Boy my dad had found in the garbage. The awkward feeling quickly dissipated, especially when one of the boys in the group said, "Wow; then I want to be a garbage man when I grow up too."

When I was a teenager, I once heard someone say my dad was *just* a garbage man. For about a year my father stopped picking up garbage and became a business-owner, but with no business training, it quickly failed. I overheard someone talk about him at an event. That word "just" meant that's all this person saw him as. They couldn't see past his job. I imagined how people would react if their garbage man stopped picking up rubbish for a few weeks, while heaps of rancid yogurt and stale milk stood at the foot of their house. Maybe in this scenario he would become more than *just* a garbage man. Maybe then he'd be called a hero.

How do you casually tell people that your father picks up trash for a living? It's hard, but not because of shame. He has never stuttered or lowered his head when stating that fact, so I haven't either. Nonetheless, people don't know what to say. When others says their father is a lawyer, soccer player, or marketing specialist, I imagine there are follow-up questions. But I've noticed questions cease when someone's job is a form of menial labor, such as janitor or house cleaner. When I say he's garbage man, it's mostly met with silence, as if the person I'm speaking to is afraid to ask the wrong thing. I get it. It's not like someone can confidently say, "So which neighborhood does he pick up garbage?" (The neighborhood where rich people throw out Chanel eyeglasses.) Nobody except one of my MFA mentors has ever asked, "Have you ever been in his garbage truck?" (He won't let me or my brother join him.)

I was at one of my first MFA residencies, having dinner with about six others, when someone from a different cohort asked, "Okay, so what job would each of you never do?"

I don't remember what each of them said, because I was coming up with a response that wouldn't make me sound like a bitch. Once my turn came along, the words came out carefully while I thought of my father urging me not to take things too seriously.

"It's difficult to answer that when you're the child of immigrants who have done jobs many people would never do. And to be honest, a lot of immigrants come to this country and do whichever job is available," I said. I didn't want to be tainted as the one who took things to heart or couldn't be included because I sucked all the fun from the room with tales verging on poverty porn. But I knew none of us at the table could have handled what my father has gone through for about three decades. My father doesn't have to wonder, *Which job do I wish my child never has to do?* He already has an answer to this question, and it didn't come to him in a hypothetical sense. The reason he has picked up garbage is so my brother and I had better options. It was a sentence that had come directly from his mouth, especially when we (mostly my brother) didn't get good grades. He didn't want us to beat up our bodies, be ridiculed, or be placed in dangerous situations like he has.

My father would mostly tell me funny stories from his job when I was a kid, and it wasn't until I got older when he began sharing the ones that put his life at risk. He didn't tell me until I was twenty-five about the gun he had pointed at him in the mid-1990s, early on when his command of English was almost nonexistent. One day, after emptying garbage into his truck from a home in Greenwich, a cop car blocked him and two policemen exited with guns pointed at him.

"Where's the bag?" one of them shouted.

My dad, in shock and frustrated that his tongue couldn't produce the questions that arose in his mind, put his hands up. One of them opened the door and asked to be shown the garbage bag.

"Bag? In back," he shouted. The officer checked the front of the garbage truck to see if he had hidden the bag in between the seat and floor, in the glove compartment, somewhere. At this point, with no "evidence" in the front seat, the police officers asked him to follow them.

He was led to one of the houses he had just scooped garbage from, and when he stepped down from the truck, the officers began to interrogate him. When they couldn't communicate, an officer called for an interpreter. In the meantime, with hand gestures and facial expressions, my dad showed them what he did. Two garbage cans were overflowing, and there was an additional black bag placed near the cans. He threw everything into the back of the garbage truck and pressed a button to squish all the contents. A Spanish-speaking officer later arrived to tell him he had destroyed a renowned painting valued at a quarter of a million dollars. When I asked him if he knew the painter's name, he said this question hadn't even crossed his mind.

The police and my father drove to the dumping grounds and threw out all the contents from the truck. In it they found the painting, crumpled up, now worth nothing. My father hadn't stolen a painting. He was convinced that it was just another bag of garbage that hadn't fit in the cans. Apparently, the homeowner had left the bagged painting by the cans so they wouldn't forget it when leaving the house, but my father had arrived to do his job. The insurers called him for weeks on end to interview him about what happened. The owner lost a painting, but my father was thankful he didn't lose his job.

On another occasion, a three-legged chair was found next to the garbage cans. He swung it inside the truck and crushed it to smithereens. The owner called the company to tell them that it wasn't garbage but an antique. His boss ended up paying eight hundred dollars for the chair, and my father vowed never to pick up anything that wasn't inside the garbage can. When chairs, boxes, and bags were left for days on end in the driveways, the owners would come out and ask him why he didn't pick them up. If they had enough time, he would tell them the story of when he had a gun pointed at him for accidentally mistaking a bagged painting for garbage.

It wasn't until he shared all these stories with me that I began to wonder how he assessed the stuff he picked up. He hadn't known there was a painting in a bag or that a chair was an antique, but what about everything else he had hauled into our home in the previous years? How did he know when something was garbage or not?

"You just know," he said.

"What do you mean, you just know? Papi, that . . . doesn't even make sense. I know you. It's not like you would dig through garbage."

"I'll give you one example. A family always threw out their stuff in white garbage bags. One day they threw out four black bags. I knew they must have done some spring cleaning. And people throw out things they may not want but others may need."

There were times when the homeowners got to know him, and even offered to give him last season's designer collection they no longer wanted.

"You know, rich women are skinny and have big feet. Just like your mom."

It seems odd, but being a garbage collector is my father's ideal job. It goes with his personality. My dad could never work in customer service because he cannot sugarcoat anything. To this day, he will tell strangers, and his children, if they're acting like fools. He was once kicked out of Wednesday-night bible study for saying gay people should be allowed to get married. He's a firm believer in the death penalty. Friendships have ended abruptly because his brutal honesty makes others uncomfortable. I have a running joke in my family that if we ever had our own reality TV show, it would be canceled after the first episode, once viewers become appalled by his non-politically-correct takes on everything. His beliefs, and his knack for voicing them, will always trump hurting someone's feelings.

Still, my dad has a penchant for conversation. He can speak to the person at a deli counter or the millionaire waiting for his car to warm up with equal ease. When he first moved to the States, he only spoke to people in Spanish. But as he began picking up garbage, he listened to the radio and learned new words. He went home and watched movies in English. When he called to try and get out of jury duty and said, "I don't speak English," the person on the line said he actually spoke the language very well. I made fun of him that day, telling him he should have just asked to speak to someone in Spanish. "I forgot that I do speak English, but not enough to judge someone, you know?" he said. Sometimes homeowners are surprised that he has such a command of English, maybe due to his brown skin and job. That's another aspect of the job. Sometimes it's just not his body that takes a beating, it's his pride too.

Just a couple of years ago, as he was entering a millionaire's property in Darien, Connecticut, the owner, a Russian man with a thicker accent than my dad's, stopped him and asked that he never back up the garbage truck farther than a specific point in his winding driveway.

"No problem, I'll stop there," he said. But the owner wasn't satisfied with his response.

"But just like you tell a child to do something, you have to explain the reason. Come here." The man pointed to a spot in front of him, urging my father to stand before him next to his luxury car. My father grabbed the garbage, put it in the truck, and got in, leaving the man waiting. From the open window my dad looked at the man and said, "Guess what? I'm not your child," then left. He laughed as he pictured the man seething. My father may pick up garbage, but he takes no shit. Fifteen minutes later, his boss called him. A man had called screaming.

"What did I do wrong, Mrs. Fields?" my dad asked.

"He asked you to do something and you didn't do it."

"He asked me to park the truck to a certain place and I did that and will do that," he said.

"But then he wanted to talk to you," she said.

"Mrs. Fields, I did as he asked. I don't have time to talk because I have more houses to do. I have to get back to work," he said.

My dad knew the homeowner would never say that he had demeaned him by calling him a child, and he wasn't going to tell his boss either. He's just kept on working and tried to avoid homeowners as much as he could, like any other day. When he told me that story, he said: "I'm glad this happened twenty years after I arrived. If I had just gotten here, I would have stepped right in front of him like a damn child. Fuckin' prick." This is why he tries not to come across any customers, and it's primarily the reason he leaves for work before five in the morning. Also, no altercations mean he will continue to receive Christmas tips.

Vivid memories from my childhood come to the fore around Christmastime every year. When I was a kid, my father would arrive home with the same shoe box, day in and day out in December. It had to be a box that could fit men's hiking boots, and my father wrapped it with thick duct tape at the end of each day, making sure its contents didn't spill out in the journey from the garbage truck to his car and to our home. He left the continuously frayed box on the dining room table. Like always, he would put his clothes in the washing machine and hop directly into the shower. Once winter came along, his brown cheeks would be perpetually red from windburn. He placed lotion on his cheeks once he got out of the shower, and his hands always stayed clean, with no bumps or bruises, as he never took his gloves off during work. Once he made sure to wash the smell off his body, he would sit down and watch television and wait for me to get home and count the end-of-the-year tips. My job was to open the envelopes stuffed in the box, take out the bills, and place them neatly in stacks with the president's face up. What intrigued me the most about our ritual was how each customer wrote out my dad's name.

At the beginning of the holiday season, my dad enclosed a Christmas card in a Ziploc bag with the stamp *Happy Holidays, from your garbage collector, Reinaldo.* When they sent in their own sparkly cards, photos of their families with Santa hats on a Caribbean island or in front of a helicopter, they wrote *Ronaldo, Roberto, Renaldo, Rinaldinho,* and *Ray* in cursive or messy handwriting. We said the wrong names out loud and mispronounced them, wondering if they did it on purpose.

The most surprising find that arrived during my childhood was an Xbox with the plastic enclosure still intact. For a moment I sat at the table and thought he had actually gone to the toy store to purchase it. But then he said, "Why do you think they threw this in the garbage?"

"Are you sure it works?"

"There's not a scratch. It was wrapped in a separate clear bag *in* the garbage can. It wasn't a mistake."

"Maybe the mom and the dad each bought one and realized it when they got home, and just threw the other one away because they're so filthy rich?" I said.

"Do you think they realized this is not the latest Xbox and just thought it would be best to throw it away?" my dad asked.

"Maybe it was a surprise for their kid and the parents got home, learned he got bad grades, and were so angry they threw it away?" I said.

"And they probably made the kid watch. And if you're bad I'll throw it in the garbage too . . . because it didn't cost me a thing," he said as he pointed at me with his index finger.

"But Papi, I'm never bad."

"You're right. Pero por si acaso nomás."

"The controls are missing. Can we go today instead of waiting for the weekend?" I knew it was the middle of the week and he was tired, but on that day I had to try.

"Vamos, before I sit down on the couch and change my mind."

Our interactions have changed slightly now that we're both adults. In January 2020, I had come back feeling defeated from my last MFA residency. The interactions with a teacher resulted in a meeting with the program director. I cried when I hadn't cried for any reason during my first three residencies. I told my husband that I only stayed to finish the program because it was my last semester. I didn't feel like sharing what had happened with my parents, especially my father. Discussing racist teachers and microaggressions with him felt like a disservice to his work. Whatever I was going through wasn't as hard as picking up strangers' garbage in the heat or freezing weather for decades.

"How was school?" he said.

"Well, más o menos. What can you do? A mix of everything, I guess."

"David told me a bit." I wondered how much my husband had shared.

"Oh, yeah?" I said. I wanted to change the subject, so I stalled and went to grab some water in the kitchen. And then suddenly I saw them. Two Beats headphones, one white oversized pair and another red, slightly skinnier version. There was also a Kindle reader with hockey stickers on it. I realized they were new finds. I grabbed them all and went to show my dad in the living room, as if they had magically appeared and he hadn't placed them in the kitchen himself.

"What's this?"

"Cuidado, don't throw them away," he said.

"I know, I know. Do they work?"

"I don't know yet. They look fine on the outside, well, except for that one," he said as he pointed to a loose headphone hanging like a dangling rope.

"But that's an easy fix. The sound, let's see if that works. I haven't had time lately, so I haven't been able to work on them. Why? You can grab a pair."

"I still have that purple pair you found a few years back, and they work just fine. The Kindle, though. Are you keeping it?"

"No, I know you like to read. You gotta set it up with your email."

"Gracias, Papi. This is great, I've been meaning to get one. Can't believe you found one."

"Aw, you should have told me. They get thrown out all the time."

My dad already knows he'll be retiring sooner than the age of sixty-five. He's a garbage man. A garbage collector. He picks up people's junk. But his father left him buildings and land in his hometown of Milagro, Ecuador. I don't want him to pick up trash until I can see the veins on his hands, and I'm sure he doesn't either. One day, when someone asks me what my father does for a living, I hope I can say: "Nothing. He's probably sitting on the beach somewhere, drinking a beer." I imagine he will forever wake up before the sun pierces the sky because he's done so for close to three decades. My father's finds are a mix of trash, treasure, and an occasional olive branch. But the smell of garbage will one day be behind him, and I know that through our screams and silence, each bag of trash he picked up was for me. I often think about how our relationship will shift once he retires. Hopefully, before then, we can find something other than garbage to bring us together.

ON DESERTION

It was early summer in Connecticut, when the days made you sweat but the arrival of night summoned the need for a sweater. I remember the day in fragments—flashes. I don't remember how the two of us, maybe twelve years old, ended up with my friend's sister and other high schoolers. I don't remember how we arrived at the quaint part of town, far from our apartment buildings. I remember we ventured there because of a boy or, in my eyes then, a man. Mila, her sister Cristina, one of her friends, and me. If Cristina were to tell it, I know she'd say we'd somehow gotten stuck with her. Once the dark of night hit, her friend was with a one-syllable-named boy, maybe Mark or Rob or Ben. Their bodies getting closer, hips and knees pointed toward each other, and we knew he'd never leave to take the three of us back to the south side of town. None of us had cash, buses didn't pass by this sidewalk-less neighborhood, and so I pictured us walking, the skin protecting our Achilles' heel rancid by the time we got back home.

Someone called for a taxi anyway, and Cristina told us we'd ditch it.

I tried to play it cool, trying to hide the already brewing remorse on my face. I prepared myself for what I was about to do because I'd never stolen from anyone. I reached down into my pocket, hoping to find a ten-dollar bill I'd forgotten was there, but I already knew there was nothing.

The black car stopped in front of us while we waited in the street.

"Holy shit," Cristina said. "I know her."

Her? I thought. I had never been in a taxi while a woman drove it. Or with a driver that wasn't a stranger. I thought we'd be ditching a man—some guy. The music from the speakers mimicked how my heart pounded all the way into my neck. In my memory, she wore a headband with intricate designs coated in orange and coils of red. Or maybe her hair was in braids. It's difficult to recall because I tried my best to avoid looking at her face. From the back seat I could see her black hands relaxed on the steering wheel. She had an accent—not a Trinidadian accent like Cristina or an accent like my Ecuadorian mom. But I knew that, like us, she had come to this country. In their banter, she mentioned being a bus driver during the school year and a taxi driver on the side. The guilt rose red on my cheeks, and I didn't want her to look at me because my eyes would surely give our intentions away. I wished she wasn't a woman. If it was a man, I was convinced my throat wouldn't feel so tight. And the driver's ease, her trust, made my body constrict. For a moment it occurred to me as Mila and I were silent in the back seat that the ruse was up. The lady would definitely know where they lived. But neither of us said a thing when she was asked to park near a building where, Cristina clarified, she'd *just* moved in with her sister and mother.

I was aware of each movement—the way the slammed doors felt too loud. My fingers looking for my pockets or somewhere on my body to rest. Cristina stayed back for a few seconds, talking about *money from my mom*, and then we walked by the one-floor apartments with peeled paint, a group of men standing by a bent tree, smoking, ending a conversation as we walked by them so they could start talking about our spaghetti straps and tight jeans. We turned a corner somewhere, and once we couldn't see the taxi, we assumed she couldn't see us. *Run*, Cristina said, barely a whisper, and we stomped each foot in front of us as if a trail of rats had scurried from the bushes.

We ran past the community center's fields, where we played with squirt guns just the summer before. The men hanging around there stopped for us too, and they shouted to keep going, egging us on to escape whatever we were running from. Their laughs became howls when Mila lost a shoe and she ran back to put it on. I was grateful for this moment of respite, when I caught a breath as I waited for her fingers to spool and unspool. I heard whoops when she finished, and I didn't dare look back, just in case the woman was chasing us and my legs would halt at the sight.

When we got to their building, we placed our hands on our knees to catch our breath, to decide on aspects of the lie. But Cristina was already thinking about the future.

"What'll I say to her in September?"

"Pay her," I panted.

She nodded, looked down, and we waited until our bodies calmed from the adrenaline. My mind drifted to the waiting game the taxi driver surely played in the idling car. I wondered how long it took for her to understand. If she got out of her car to ask the group of men where some teenagers went. I wondered about her loss, and none of our gains. Her loss of—not just money—but time. I wondered if she had children, and if she was single like Mila and Cristina's mom. The other call she could have answered instead of ours. I wondered how many people had done this to her, and I hoped she would remember our faces because we were her first and last ditch. Even though I knew, deep down, as the latch bolt clinked behind us, that we weren't the only ones.

A LEGACY OF BONE

In the beginning, Mr. Damon is like all the homeowners my mother cleans for. He doesn't have a set schedule, lives in one of the wealthiest towns in Fairfield County, says just a few words to her whenever she arrives, and then promptly leaves her alone with his dust bunnies. Sometimes his platinum-blonde wife greets my mom, and then she strides to her car and maybe, possibly, goes to have some salad and tea for lunch at Lord & Taylor. At least that's what my mom thinks. I remember going there once or twice, only seeing her as she left wearing a fur coat, wondering why the white people my mother cleans for don't seem to believe in purchasing blinds. While there, my mother doesn't let me lift a finger. She leaves me on the leather couch, remote control in hand, and tells me to watch whatever I want until the house shines. When I'm young, I think it's because I'm a nuisance, because once she trusted me enough to play in a home's pool and then I threw up in a mud room. For years I don't realize that it's because she doesn't want me to feel like I was born to clean.

In our car on the way to mansions, I usually catch glimpses of someone going on about their day within the warmth of their house as my mother weaves through back roads between Greenwich, Darien, and Westport. There are large Cape Cod–style houses with Labrador retrievers sunbathing on flawless grass, or the occasional stone-veneer facade with a matching fence and three-car garage. A few houses take a stab at Greek Revival with white columns in the front yard and a pendant light between them that's kept on throughout the day. The windows are always wide, letting in all the sun, letting me peer in and wonder what their lives are like. From time to time when the car halts at a stop sign, I see dwellers reading the newspaper in the living room, a man and woman talking with a wide kitchen island between them, or an older woman wearing a pastel crimson sweater while talking on the phone—sometimes I even see shirtless backs from the second-floor bathroom. I look away fast, embarrassed for them, wondering if they realize their lives are being laid bare.

A year after my mother cleans Mr. Damon and the once-model's house every couple of weeks, he starts changing. His skin looks drier, his face gaunt, and one morning before he leaves my mother alone in the house, she sees the track marks weaving around his right arm. She doesn't know that's what they're called, just that someone shouldn't have puntos negros on their arms. On another occasion she finds a tiny bag of white stuff within the maze of bedsheets. My mother is naive, and she takes it with her to ask my dad what it could possibly be. She crosses the town line from Westport to our apartment in Norwalk, and when my dad sees it he laughs, then grabs it and throws the contents down the toilet. *What if a cop had stopped you?* he says as he shakes his head. My dad knows that people like Mr. Damon go to rehab, while people like my mom get arrested.

A few months later, the wife calls. There was an intervention, but something happened in the basement before he left. *When you come over today, can you take a peek downstairs? Let me know if you can handle it. If not, please call someone else. I don't want to see the mess when I come back. Throw away everything if you have to. I'll pay you more, of course. Oh, you're a godsend. I have to run some errands. Talk soon.*

My mother says yes because you don't say no to extra money, but once she gets there and peeks from the top of the basement stairs, she knows she can't handle it. She calls my father, and he urges her not to touch anything. He'll be there with extra cleaning supplies and gloves.

My mother recalls the smell of lingering smoke—days old—saturating the walls. There are dozens of syringes, spoons, white dust, lighters, shards of broken glass, torn paintings, a table, and chairs tipped over. Since the basement is used as a storage room, there are old modeling photos of the wife, now smeared in specks of blood, more of it dotting clothes found in disarray. My father is a garbage man, and on that afternoon he also becomes a one-man biohazard cleanup crew. They tell me about it on that very same day when they come home, as much as they can share with a kid. *How sad*, my mom says, *all that money wasted away on drugs*. I don't remember what my dad says or what I say. I probably ask them if they plan on going back. *Of course*, my mom would have said.

They don't finish that same day but go back on the weekend to leave the basement with no evidence of drug use. I wonder how much of a burden has been lifted off his wife's shoulders. Not having to endure bearing witness to the aftermath. To sign a check and have the visual remnants disappear. None of us know then, as my mother scrubs, as my father helps, that my mother won't be able to open a can of olives by the time she's fifty. Her knuckles will deform as if the bones have become bolts due to arthritis, useless for opening and shutting. She'll stop cleaning and decide only to babysit because the stench of Clorox will become too much, strangers' houses too demanding to handle by herself. And when I'm older, residing in Fairfield County, I'll think about her on my way to work, hands clasped on the steering wheel; remember how a man once grabbed my hands and said "manos de gatita," referring to how they resembled a paw's soft-pink carpal pads. Hands that my mother wanted me to have when she would only let me hold a remote.

After the couple's divorce, the woman finds a new place while he keeps the house with the basement. My mother may be the only witness of their dissolving marriage, and she keeps on cleaning both their houses. When Mr.

Damon comes back from rehab, he still calls my mother to wipe the floors, throw bleach in the tub, make his bed. My mom never mentions his drug bouts, not even with her eyes. That's why they both call her time and time again. She'd already seen their lives unravel. She's there to leave the house spotless, and whatever isn't salvageable, she throws away.

BUT WHERE ARE YOU REALLY FROM?

What I want to say:

From the syntax of Spanglish sentences. The tilde, umlaut, dieresis. The strips of sapote I devoured yesterday still stuck between my teeth, irking my gums. My father's latent rage. Nowhere. From whichever sound lava makes when it froths into the ocean. Larkspur. The brown of overripe pineapples. My ancestors. The collision of comet Shoemaker-Levy 9 with Jupiter. An incessant twitch on the left eyelid. Plantains, definitely plantains. A tongue touching the hard palate when emphasizing a double *r*.

What I answer:

I was born in _____, but I've lived in _____ most of my life.

MY CHOSEN FAMILY

Getting married and having kids seemed like an impossibility for years. The former because I assumed it odd that in a world with eight billion people, I could find someone I would want to spend day in and day out with. You would think that the overwhelming options would make me feel better, but it just made me want to crawl back into my shell of existence. The latter *is* impossible because I don't want to have kids, and I felt like all the men I met wanted a human to come from them, something I'm not willing to provide.

I've always wanted to love, be in love, and be loved. I want that weird love. Love the way an owl curves its neck without fissuring tendons in the blanket of the night. Love the way wonderment hits you at an intersection where the green, yellow, and red traffic lights are all turned on. Love the way the *ñ* sounds on the tongue. Love in which he makes sure I come before him. Love in two languages. The love and the lack of resistance when learning a new language because you want to learn not just what a word means but how it feels. *Impossible,* I thought.

I kissed my now husband an hour after I met him. I agreed to leave Connecticut and cross the border into New York fifteen minutes after we met. Just like that. As if I was sure he wasn't evil. I saw him before he saw me. His hair was cut close to his scalp. It was October, but his skin looked freshly tan, as if he had recently returned from vacation in a warm place. He was skinny, with a chiseled chin and eyes that halt. Even now, years later, I lie next to him in bed and contemplate his eyes. Sometimes I'm sure they're tropical-forest green; on certain days they're a striking teal, and on others they're cloaked in gray. My concerns with safety that night? Out the car window on the way to White Plains.

I enjoy talking about words with him. Words from Ecuador, words from his native Costa Rica. We share the same colonized tongue with deviations. Well, and another one that colonizes. One day he calls me to say he's picking me up ahorita. Me, I imagine waiting seconds, maybe a couple of minutes, tops. And there I am, waiting half an hour later, wondering where he is. We figure out that *ahorita* for him means "later," unraveling the only definition I've ever had for it, killing its meaning.

Teach me a word, I say.

Teach me a term I don't know.

Explain the meaning of a word in the place you got that scar on your lip.

We discuss why the word for "popcorn" differs in almost every Latin American country.

Poporopo in Guatemala
Pochocho in Argentina
Pipoca in Bolivia
Crispetas in Colombia
Canchita in Peru
Palomitas in Costa Rica
Canguil in Ecuador

I prefer the Ecuadorian version, the way the vowels after the *g* soften it.

We talk in English and Spanish. We talk in Spanglish. When we're together three years and he says a word I've never heard, I wonder what other definitions he'll teach me in the future. We fight in both languages. Our bodies fuck in English but make love in Spanish. Sorry, you can only understand if you know both languages. I revise his homework for errors in English. He draws a portrait of me in art class. He's a visual learner, a photographer, a dreamer, a graphic designer.

On our first date, not the night we met but the night we plan, he takes me to a fancy restaurant and wears a button-up shirt. It's weird to be on a date with him. I thought I'd be a sure fuck and he'd be done with me. He's too hot for me. In the years to come, women will go up to him at clubs while I'm standing next to him; they'll hit on him at work and compliment his eyes. People will ask him at the grocery line: *Do you know who you look like? That guy. What's his name? From* Grey's Anatomy. I'll see women stare at us while whispering to each other and disbelief in their eyes. It might be the second or third date, but I ask him: *Why are you not an asshole? With those looks you should be a pretentious and pompous fucker.* He's honest. He tells me he used to be like that. Until he arrived to the United States and couldn't speak in English. It humbled him—having to pay rent at fifteen, working in the ice of January washing cars when the sun sets by five. His looks couldn't help him then.

Maybe it's because we meet when I'm twenty-three and he's twenty-two, but the first few months we fuck like we're on a deadline before one of us has to suddenly leave for an indeterminate amount of time. We spend too much money on hotels. One night the fire alarm rings and fire-fighters show up to check our hotel room while I hide naked in the bathroom. On another night, we open the door of a hotel room to find a half-naked sleeping couple already on the bed. He closes the door ever so tenderly, so they never realize two strangers walked in on them. The moment stays with me. How you can live for years without knowing someone and then seeing them at their most vulnerable. I'm not referring to the nakedness but the fact that they were sleeping, resting, feeling safe in the oblivion of their bodies. He runs to the office, and I trail behind as he screams at the receptionist about getting our money back.

Do you know what could have happened?
If they were awake?
You wanted me to get in a fucking fight with a stranger?
What the fuck, man?
Is this how you run a business?
You're lucky they were fucking sleeping.
Anything could have happened.
We're never coming back.

I was lost in oblivion before him, I think. Until he came and woke me up.

My husband doesn't speak much. He's shy. His cheeks redden easily. I tell him the voice he uses in Spanish sounds different than the one in English. He says the same about me. When he's with other Costa Ricans, I can hardly understand the conversation. The words ring out at a different pace, as if he's a different person. Once I asked him to tell me something sexy, but in Spanish. Just because anything sounds better in a Romance language. He said: Quiero devorarte toda. "I want to devour all of you." I laughed until tears sprouted from my eyes. He was mocking a Wisin y Yandel song. We still say that to each other as an inside joke, as an ode to perreo sucio.

I don't remember when I told him I didn't want to have children. Maybe that's a good thing. That it was like pulling a Band-Aid and not mending a wound. I don't remember my words or what language I used. He said it was fine. Just like that, fine. As if I was asking whether it was okay to go to the movie theater even though it's hailing. Sure. Fine. I do know, even though I have no recollection of it, that I told him that I understood he could change his mind at any time. Just like he needed to understand, maybe one day, to his surprise and my surprise, maybe I'd like to have a kid. Hardly feasible, but not impossible.

It sounds ridiculous, but I think we were bound to meet. I left Norwalk, Connecticut, in 2004. He moved there in 2006, and he roamed the halls of the high school I only finished my freshman year in. We would have crossed paths. Maybe we wouldn't have noticed each other, or maybe we would have played hooky together. We're glad we'll never know.

We accept the love we think we deserve.
  Aceptamos el amor que creemos merecer.
  Stephen Chbosky in *The Perks of Being a Wallflower*

I hate that people have to explain why they don't want children. There somehow needs to be a justification. It can never be because I don't want to. It can never be because you love your life.

I

       Just

           Don't

               Want

                    Children

                              &

                    There

               Won't

          Be

      A

Because

In the Dominican Republic, we stayed in a resort where no children were allowed. I felt guilty at first, because I had avoided resorts for my entire adult life. But he insisted all he wanted to do, for the first time in his life, was lounge around without worrying about cooking or driving or parking. It makes me feel even guiltier confessing how much we enjoyed it. Living, just for a few days, in a place without crying children. How he kept surprising everyone when he spoke Spanish because they thought he was a gringo. We read books while drinking mojitos, waking before everyone else to see the sun rise. I'd look over as the salt dried on his skin that left swirls, hoping he'll be there, years from now, my chosen family, to hear new words coming out of my mouth, to conjoin them with his, and make sentences, paragraphs, books out of our lives.

DRIVING BY GREAT ISLAND
ON CHILLY EVENINGS

I'm in the neighborhood a few times per month, mostly on weekend nights, to make a hundred bucks by taking care of other people's children. It's an easy job—at least in the houses I go back to. If a kid throws a full-body tantrum and refuses to sleep at the time their parents deem appropriate, or tells me I smell like rice, I simply don't return. I don't need the money, although I want it for my savings fund. My route toward this enclave traverses by the Rings End bridge and an entrance to Great Island, which was listed for sale at $120 million in 2018. I continue onto Long Neck Point Road, and from there the view of the private island is so vast the Long Island Sound remains hidden. The pristine grass is surrounded by the property's ornamental steel fence, one that may have been installed in the middle of the last century. Vines interweave between the hundreds of pickets; certain sections have more rust than others, where the black steel has given way to the color of mud.

My mom, who works in the area as a full-time baby-sitter, sees a deer on top of the fence one day, trying to get onto the island property, rocking, as if trying to pull away from an invisible noose around its neck. It isn't until she enters her employer's house that she understands the deer is caught, maybe in the last moments of its life, struggling to survive until its bodily functions cease. It's the only time my mother has been a witness to such a scene, but her boss tells her it happens often. Sometimes when Animal Control arrives, the deer are dead, tongues sticking out, their bodies slumped over thorns and vines, the decomposition barely starting, and the workers are in a hurry to remove it so neighborhood children don't learn the word "impalement" before school.

Each kid has their own ritual before bed. For some it's sipping milk and eating apples for dessert. Others want to be read a book before bed, while some say *'night* and bang their bedroom door hard enough to make it clear I'm only there because their parents don't trust them to be alone. I read two stories if the kids pick short ones, or I lie and make up the story if I know they can't read. A few surprise me with a hug before I leave the night-light on. I assume the warmth comforts them as they enter the peace of sleep. I never mention the dead deer, of course. But once they are in bed, maybe fake sleeping but at least in bed, I let the dog out in the yard and my mind deviates to stags. If it's a night that only requires a light sweater, I follow the dog, throw a ball around, and stare at the stars. There aren't any streetlights, and I see thousands of them, glistening, wondering which ones are dying, collapsing onto themselves until all that's left is the light of their past. Sometimes I spot a doe and its fawn, or maybe a lone deer skipping away from the danger of barks, toward Great Island. Shushing the dog doesn't help because the deer are already escaping toward what they assume is salvation, away from a dog that would never bite, away from me— not knowing the fear I hold for them—the continuous crunch of leaves in unison with the whoosh of adrenaline beating within my ears. I hope they jump high, their hind limbs barely meeting the fence finials, and with a swoop it's done. Maybe they end with a scrape, but not a cut, no blood, no impalement. I'm glad I'm there only at night, the dark hiding failed leaps.

After a quick goodnight with tipsy parents, small talk as a form of etiquette before I accept a check they don't write my name on, only "Cash," I make sure to drive slowly on the road. Over the years, I've halted for opossums on moonless nights. Foxes have flashed their eyes as they've tread away in silence. The high-beam headlights are on so I don't take a life. Most of all, I avoid looking toward the fence surrounding Great Island, hoping it's not the night I see a doe that didn't make the jump. I wonder, though, if it would matter if I did see one, since my mind has created a scene of it anyway, since I know it will continue to happen, long after I stop coming to this neighborhood and once all the kids I tuck into bed forget who I am.

THE NEWLYWED GAME

If I had known I needed to take off my shoes and walk through a metal detector, I never would have worn high heels. My outfit felt more like a costume—I seldom wore below-the-knee skirts or my amber-colored high heels on a typical Thursday at nine a.m. But this was no typical day. I became even more aware of it as the security guard pointed to the waiting room and I grabbed my husband's hand to walk alongside him, surprised to feel his palm damp like just-licked chapped lips. The rectangular lobby of the William R. Cotter Federal Building in Hartford, Connecticut, could pass for a bank's interior, except security was heightened and long rows of chairs were stationed back to back, while the people behind the glass-plated information box were government officials. We decided to sit near the door that paved the way for the rest of our lives, which is where most people sat in their best attire: a Black woman with a leopard dress, a Latino in jeans and dress shoes, and a red-haired man with a scruff wearing an open-collar shirt. Our forced smiles and wary faces did little to hide our impatience. Some were there for the marriage interview—just like us—and others were surely counting down the minutes until the painstaking naturalization interview.

It dawned on me that maybe none of us wanted to be there. Maybe most of us were there because we felt we had no other choice. I was there because I loved my husband, not because I wanted to be questioned by a stranger about everything from our meet cute to how we went about our daily lives.

The door swung open and a petite woman appeared in the same uniform as all the other federal employees who surrounded us: white shirt, black pants, and a face devoid of emotion. She said a name, and a couple walked in with their lawyer, a woman who led the way in a bright red blazer. We were a few rows across from them, and in the moments before they disappeared, I was convinced she was telling them last-minute pointers. While they were sitting, her voice had been inaudible, but her mouth did not rest while she flittered her fingers and hands as if painting a canvass. The couple continuously nodded in agreement, with their chins almost touching their chests. When they could not suppress the worry anymore, their eyes drifted from her to the floor, where they remained. We were all awaiting, whether with lawyers or alone, for the resounding decisions that would consolidate or fracture our lives in the United States.

Minutes, then half an hour, and eventually an hour later, officers continued to stop by the waiting room and introduce themselves to interviewees before leading them down the secluded hallway.

"How are you feeling?" my husband asked. By then we had been staring at the clock for close to two hours.

"Good, I guess. Pretty sure they're making us wait just so we can get more and more nervous."

"Yeah, that's what they want."

A man sprinted to the door when a burly officer said his name so loudly people raised their heads in silent shock. Once they were out of sight, it seemed like we all let out a sigh of relief that he wouldn't be the one interrogating us.

"I think being with a lawyer would have made me more jittery, you know? It would have made everything more serious," I confessed.

The truth was that we didn't have the funds to pay a lawyer the three grand he had requested to fill out the application and accompany us to the interview. So I told my husband *I* would be his lawyer. Throughout the process of petitioning for David's permanent residency and sending out the paperwork to US Citizenship and Immigration Services (USCIS), I tried to remain confident. Even during the drive to the courthouse, I had attempted to convince myself that it would be like a game show on television. It wasn't too far-fetched to view it this way when in the early 2000s, US officials uncovered dozens of marriages that were only real on paper through, of course, "Operation Newlywed Game." The officer would be the host, and while we wouldn't win a cash prize at the end, my husband would receive his green card. I knew it wasn't a game, but this helped to calm me down as we approached the moment we'd been preparing for.

David sat beside me with a blue button-down shirt, his light blue eyes staring at our intertwined hands. His feet moved up and down, quick and shaky. Before he could respond to my comment about the lawyer, another door opened and a white man, blond, a little over six feet tall, called out my husband's name.

"David Sánchez?"

The officer's white cheeks were slightly puffy, and his honey-brown eyes stared at us as he motioned with a plump hand to follow him down the hallway. The three offices on each side of the corridor had clear glass for walls. The interviewees had their backs to us, fixated on the immigration officers with their spines and heads fully straight in nervous attention. I wondered if this was how interrogation rooms looked like at my local police station. At first glance, it looked like we'd entered a principal's office, but then my eyes spotted the camera lens with a red light on top of his computer. We were being filmed from the moment we stepped into the room. We sat and edged the chairs closer to his desk, and he asked us to lift our right hands and vow to say nothing but the truth.

This was it.

We had been married for less than a year, known each other for five, and David had been in the country without papers for a little more than a decade. The moment had come to present his case, to prove he hadn't paid me thousands of dollars to pretend to be his wife, to show that our marriage was real. I was confident. We had spent weeks in mock interviews at our kitchen table; our marriage was consummated and backed up with the paperwork to prove it. I was ready for the questions. Until the officer uttered the first one.

"Ms. Buitron, there's a discrepancy in your last name between your passport and birth certificate. Did you know that?"

My husband and this stranger ogled me. It had been twenty-seven years, and I'd never had a serious issue traveling to any country, even when I'd shown both of my passports. The Ecuadorian one listed my father's and mother's last name, as is customary in most Latin American countries, but the blue one from the United States had only my father's last name. I figured this was because children in the states only received their father's last name on their birth certificates. I was a kid the first time I had a passport, and I continued to renew it as a teenager and adult just as my name had appeared on my first US passport.

"When you get a new passport, it has to match exactly with what your birth certificate says." I nodded. He said this to me like I'd been carrying on a separate identity through false names my entire life. But I yielded. Fine, whatever; I wanted to get to the important part.

"I need to see your IDs." We handed over our IDs, and he turned both of them around and looked at me.

"Ms. Buitron, did you notify the State of Connecticut that you recently moved?"

I was under oath, and I told him the truth. I had not. In that moment, David stared at me in disbelief and the officer began reprimanding me. David's license had our updated address on the back; the back of my license was blank. We hadn't even started the official marriage interview, and my identity had already been questioned.

"You have to do this right away. Tomorrow. Do you understand?"

"Yes," I said.

By then, I was sure the interview would last a lot longer than I had expected. I was not completely persuaded at that moment that we should have hired a lawyer for the adjustment of status process, but this changed immediately with his next announcement.

"Before we start, I just have to inform you both that I cannot make a yes or no decision today."

David and I quickly looked at each other in dismay. I massaged my temple with my thumb, trying to ease my sudden headache. Devastated, but not wanting to give him the pleasure of seeing me cry, I asked the officer why.

"The translator wrote a certification letter for David's birth certificate but forgot to sign it. Therefore, the paperwork is incomplete. Incomplete means I can't approve or dismiss his case. You'll have to fix that after."

As a professional translator, I had decided that it would be a conflict of interest for me to translate my husband's documents as I petitioned for him to acquire legal residency in the United States on my behalf. I had contacted a translator I had worked with at a prior translation agency, and David and I had not caught that his signature was missing when we sent out the massive wad of paperwork to the US government.

We hadn't even started the questions about our marriage, and already there would be no solution, no sigh of relief. I wanted to scream, but the officer began to prod us with questions.

"So, how'd you two meet?"

David and I met in the middle of a street. After a night of dancing, I stood outside a bar after one a.m. once the bouncer had forced everyone out. A friend and I hung around talking with others. She blurted out in front of an acquaintance that I should talk to the handsome guy we were ogling from afar. No; I would roll my eyes at someone who came up to me in the middle of the street, and why would I ever go up to a man without the loud music to dim the possible rejection? I shrugged her off, but the acquaintance saw who we were eyeing and in a matter of minutes arrived with a man with vivid blue eyes, olive skin, and a shaved head. *David, meet Victoria. Victoria, meet David.* And then she left. After ten minutes, he had convinced me to cross state lines from Connecticut into New York. I'm fully aware of the danger of strangers, and there was no supernatural force that convinced me when I looked into his eyes that he would become my husband. Instead, his quiet voice and my surprise when he spoke Spanish made me trust him more than I should have trusted any man I'd just met.

David took me out to a fancy restaurant in Stamford, Connecticut, on our first date. His tiny left earring sparkled from the candlelight, and at times he blushed, specks of red flushing his cheeks. It was interesting to be on a date with someone I had already kissed in the back seat of a friend's car. We were physically attracted to each other, but I wanted to get to know him beyond that. A few minutes into our conversation, we spoke about our past lives, before we immigrated to the United States.

"How many people live in Costa Rica?" I asked.

"About four million, I think."

"That's it? Just four million. Wow."

"Yeah, we're a tiny country."

"So small, though. There are four million people just in Guayaquil. Can I take out my phone and check?" I didn't want to be rude. But there we were, on our phones checking the demographics about our birth countries, which led us to share memories about our families back home. What we missed, what we didn't, words comfortably spilling from our mouths. No awkwardness, no weird silence, and suddenly I was sad the night was ending while we shared a crème brûlée for dessert.

On our second date, David told me that he was undocumented. He sighed heavily right before he shared it with me, as if this would determine whether there would be any further make-out sessions in his Jeep. But I shrugged. He wasn't the first undocumented person I had met, and I knew he wouldn't be the last. I had friends and family members who couldn't do what I did: Leave the country, get Connecticut health insurance, risk speeding. David followed his confession with his hopes for the future: to be able to drive with a license and attend college.

"Ms. Buitron, what's your husband's status?"

I supposed it was a trick question. I wasn't taken aback that he was just focused on me from the beginning of the interview. Most of the online forums we scoured said that the officers put the pressure on the petitioner instead of the person being petitioned for US residency.

"He's undocumented."

"No, he's not. Ms. Buitron, you don't even know your husband's status?"

"He has DACA, but he's still technically undocumented."

"But he has DACA, so technically he's not."

For a second, I wanted to spit in his face. In 2012, Deferred Action for Childhood Arrivals (DACA) was enacted, and people like my husband who came to the United States as children could obtain a Social Security number and work permit. But the recipients didn't cease to be undocumented. There was no next step or application form in which they could apply for US residency. The biannual work permits David received could be rescinded at any moment. The only reason David was in front of this government official applying for a green card was because of the privilege tied to marrying me. Many undocumented individuals, whether with the benefit of DACA or not, have no real path toward citizenship unless they marry a US citizen. Plenty of them don't even have this option. DACA couldn't protect him.

There was a time, before I met David, when I had thought that any undocumented person could just get married to a US citizen and their problems would be solved. A hairdresser who I had known since I was a child mentioned one day, as she washed my scalp, that her husband was on vacation. When I asked why she hadn't gone with him, she confessed that she couldn't leave the United States. She had been married to him for almost a decade. Why was her paperwork taking so long?

"There is no paperwork. There's nothing I can do," she said.

"But you came by plane," I clarified.

"Yes, but I came in with a false passport. Coming in with a fake passport is just like crossing the border." She said those words as if she was surrendering. Each lawyer told her the same thing. She would have to leave the country, ask for forgiveness, be banned for a decade or more, and then *maybe* she could return. I was shocked. She reminded me how lucky I was. David had arrived to the United States with a tourist visa and had overstayed. The US government had given him permission to enter the country and knew he had never left.

"How did David arrive to the United States?"

"Via plane at the Bradley International Airport in Hartford."

"Who did he come with?

"No one. He came by himself."

"Who took him to get his tourist visa?"

"His grandmother."

"What are David's mom's and dad's names?"

I had memorized the answers to these questions. David's father had never been in his life. The last time he remembers seeing him was when his grandmother scoured San José, Costa Rica, to get a signature for David to leave the country. His mother died during childbirth when he was five years old. He was passed from grandma to aunt, then to another aunt, and finally back to this grandma during childhood. When he was fifteen, his grandmother told him he'd be moving to Connecticut. David arrived to the United States, unaware of the myriad ways it would affect his life, and began working at a car wash after school.

"Does he have any siblings?"

"Explain a normal weekday of your life."

"What car does David drive?"

"Name all the places where he has worked."

"When is his birthday?"

"What do you do for fun?"

Fun for us has always been exploring. About six months after we met, we took our first trip together. Before he met me, and without DACA or a license, David had gone on a trip to Florida via train. He slept in a capsule, more comfortable there than if he had taken a quick plane ride. But this time he showed his crisp Connecticut driver's license, and whispered to me how afraid he was to end up deported on a separate plane. His light skin was paler than I'd ever seen before, and his hands shivered until we sat on the plane seats. But we were able to arrive to Florida and lie on the sand and paddleboard with manatees surrounding us. The next trip was to California, where we kayaked and enjoyed it so much we bought a kayak for ourselves back home. On that same trip, we drove to Las Vegas, where we hardly drank but danced, saw shows on the strip, ziplined above water fountains, and lounged by massive pools.

David's own version of fun is drifting, a sport where you slide a car at high speeds around a race track. The first time he took me, I clawed the bottom of my seat as the car swerved. It was like a roller coaster he could control. David used the speed and the adrenaline rush to drift away from his worries—to do on a race track what is illegal anywhere else.

David couldn't escape the worries that came with being undocumented. Half his body was in the shadows, while the other glistened in the sunlight. The work permit wasn't permanent. Every two years he had to drive to New York, get fingerprints done, and pass a background check to renew DACA. There were certain aspects in which he remained a sub-resident. He enrolled in college but was not allowed to receive financial aid or take out a loan. He could only afford two classes per semester. His lawyer continuously reminded him to make sure he never received a parking ticket, much less a speeding ticket. It was imperative for him to do his taxes every year, continue to go to school, and not get fired from any job. What could for some become an anecdote, a simple hurdle in life, for him could become a challenge to depict his worthiness to become a US citizen in the future.

"How did he propose?"

My response was the only semi-lie I uttered. There were two proposals, but I omitted the first one.

After experiencing hit-and-runs, arguments, the deaths of relatives, and job changes, I knew this was the man I wanted to wake up to every morning. I asked him one day how he envisioned his future and he said, "Living near the beach with you and our dog." Simple yet profound, traits of his personality.

Eventually, even family and friends began to ask us, sometimes in subtle ways and other times as directly as possible, when we were going to get married. "Soon," we would both say. We wanted to, but our bank accounts made only a trip to City Hall affordable. Soon, though, lawyers began to ask us about our wedding plans with more urgency than my mother.

By 2016, four years after we met, we'd discussed living together. One night, David and I were watching a debate between the Republican presidential candidates. "If any of these men win, DACA won't exist anymore," I told him. We met with different lawyers that week. When we spoke to them, they all arrived at the same two conclusions. For one, if we had been together as long as we had and already knew we wanted to be together, we should marry as soon as possible. "You never know who might win the upcoming election, and you might not want to take that risk," one of them told us.

The other consensus was that David wouldn't have a hard time becoming a permanent resident once we were married. He'd entered the country with a tourist visa and overstayed. David had never been in trouble with the law. He had a full-time job. He paid his taxes every year, was going to college, and interned as a graphic designer for a nonprofit that helped the relatives of the victims of 9/11. There was nothing from his past that could put the process of petitioning his residency in jeopardy. We needed to discuss among ourselves whether we wanted to get married before the 2016 election.

After meeting with lawyers over cheap Cabernet Sauvignon, we talked about the future. There were things we had already decided on: We were dog people and not cat people, we would retire near the beach, and we promised never to go to sleep angry. I knew, without external factors piling up, that he loved me for me and not a green card. I had long been wary of finding someone who I could not only withstand but wanted to wake up to, discuss the plots of films with, enjoy the silence in museums and sip cocktails on the beach with. I wanted a bilingual man, one who spoke to me in Spanish and English, who didn't mind dancing salsa, someone who filled my days with laughter—a man who was kind without trying to be. I couldn't imagine having inside jokes in just one language, unable to go to concerts by Maná and The Killers without my partner understanding both lyrics.

We belonged together. Nonetheless, we were confronted with marital questions that not many couples face. Were we going to get married in 2016 before the election, or would we wait and hope the new president didn't end DACA? Did we need to hire a lawyer for the adjustment of status process? Could our budget allow for a wedding *and* the adjustment of status application fees? How long would the green card take to arrive? What would happen if he were deported? Where would we live if this were to happen, since we don't share the same nationalities? The lack of romantic questions annoyed me. But we also cared more about our marriage than the wedding day.

David and I decided on a small reception and picked out the rings at the mall. There was only one thing we didn't do together, due to my request. In order to have some pre-wedding normalcy, I asked him to officially propose when I was least expecting it. I just wanted a surprise. A moment stripped away from the tediousness of safeguarding his stay in the country. By the time he got on one knee on a New York City rooftop in June, we had already sent out the wedding invitations, I had gotten my dress, and the location was booked.

Some of the questions were in logical order; others were tossed out arbitrarily to catch us off guard. "What did Victoria study in college?" was followed by "What did you two do last weekend?" Then he asked a question we imagined would take no time to clarify.

"Why don't you have a checking account together?"

"I don't know, but we do have a savings account together," I said.

"How do you pay your rent?"

"Victoria pays for it through her checking account. I transfer my half to her every month," my husband said with the utmost confidence.

"I've never heard of that before. Wouldn't it be easier to have just one account together?"

"I don't know. To be honest, we never even discussed it. We just stayed with the checking accounts we've had since we were single and created a savings account for the future," David said.

"Are you afraid he's going to see the purses you buy or something?" he said with a slight chuckle. He leaned back in his chair, relishing his joke. I was sure the words were said to spite me, because the records showed my income outpaced my husband's.

"All of our utilities are included in our rent. When I pay the landlord with a check, David just texts me his portion."

That my husband texted me money confounded him even more. He didn't seem that old, but this cellphone feature seemed like a foreign concept to him. Even worse, it elicited doubt in his voice. But he quickly changed the topic.

"What do you fight about?"

"We don't really fight that much. I'm not one to get angry or upset," David said. This was true. In the years that we'd known each other, there had been only a few times that I'd seen him upset. David had never raised his voice at me, and would show his anger by calling me Victoria instead of the usual "babe." His angriest moment came when someone smashed their vehicle into his car and left the scene. He wasn't even worried about the dent, but he imagined it could become an immigration woe down the line.

"I'm usually the one that gets upset. But they're petty things . . . and I eventually realize they're not that important."

"Can you give me an example?"

"I don't know . . . um . . . when I tell him something and he completely forgets. He doesn't write things down and then asks me why I didn't remind him. That's annoying. Or that I have to beg him to go to the doctor."

"And you, Mr. Sánchez?"

"Mmm, nothing really. She can be intense sometimes about certain things, but we get over it."

Our lukewarm answers didn't satisfy him.

"You're telling me you hardly fight and you also don't have a checking account together?"

David responded with more details this time; he took out his phone, probably to show him the monthly transfers he makes to me, but it all seemed like a dream sequence. My worries soon eclipsed his voice. The officer was holding our future lives hostage. Rapid thoughts popped up in my mind. We shouldn't have planned our honeymoon two months after the interview—it now appeared to be a cocky move. Would we go back home to our small apartment and stop worrying about deportation, or would David's process to request permanent residency extend past the ten-year mark? The officer didn't believe that I'd promised my body to this man, that we'd bickered about what to name our dog once all this was resolved, and that, for the last five years, I've never spent more than two weeks away from him. Our marriage was a farce, and I had to do something to make it real in the eyes of this stranger.

"Excuse me. Where are the pictures?"

I cut off David in mid-sentence, and they both looked astonished that I had spoken out of turn. But the question erupted from my lips as soon as I remembered that all the forums mentioned the officer always asked questions about the photographs.

"What photos? You didn't walk in with any photos today, ma'am."

"No, we didn't. But we sent more than a hundred photos with dates and descriptions with the application. Where are they?"

He looked at the folder in front of him, one side rose for about six inches; the other looked like about half the breadth of the adjacent stack.

"I think it's in there," I said as I pointed to the slim stack. "There's a beige envelope there. It looks like the envelope we sent."

The officer began to slip the manila envelope out of the folder, never taking his eyes off me. He thrust open the flap, turned the envelope upside down, and the last five years spilled out like milk. David caught a few photos before they fell off the desk. The officer rolled his eyes.

"The person that organizes this folder has to put all the evidence on the right. All the normal paperwork on the left. Sorry about that," he said.

The apology was enough for us to take advantage of the situation, and we hovered off the chairs, pointing to our lives on the desk.

"That's David's grandma at our wedding," I said. David grabbed three photos from our wedding day, careful to pick ones with different guests.

"Oh, and here are our engagement photos," I said. I had on a bright green dress and David and I had walked into a field, where we had to pry ticks from our legs. In order to show the length of our relationship, I moved the photos around like puzzle pieces until I found three in which the season, our hairstyles, and weight differed from how we appeared before him. Years ago, I had gotten a pixie haircut, to David's surprise and dismay. In the years I've known my husband, he's had a clean shave, a beard almost touching his collarbone, and a mustache.

One photo stood out from among the pile. I'm in a striped dress and my then-boyfriend is in a sleeveless T-shirt on a Florida beach with a pink sun setting behind us. David was sent to a conference by his employer just a few months after we met. "It's not really a vacation, but we can get in the warm sea in the afternoons. No pointy rocks or brown water. Come with me," he said. We rented a car when we arrived and drove to different beaches, and he tried surfing for the first time, an endeavor that left a tender bruise on the left side of his torso. When he asked that I join him and I said no, that I feared the ocean more than I adored it, he left me with my book on the sand and walked away—calm, quiet, and understanding.

David's voice brought me back to the officer's interrogation. I had never heard him speak as fast, with so much determination. He usually lacked words, unlike me, and he showed me a side of him I'd never seen before.

"This couple drove from New Jersey. Victoria's best friend flew from Ecuador. These are all of our friends from Connecticut. And that's Victoria's aunt who flew in from Arkansas," David said, almost out of breath.

I followed his lead. "This photo is of us kayaking in California. The other is skiing in the Berkshires. That's us hiking in the Catskills of New York. I don't remember the dates right now, but I wrote them on the back," I said.

"You can both take a seat now."

He asked us a few more questions about the photos. In the subsequent minutes, he eased up, and his chair was rocking back and forth while his arms hung loosely at his side. He was no longer questioning us but talking to us. That was it. All he had to see were our naive twenty-five-year-old faces.

"Alright guys, everything pans out," he said. "You'll be fine."

"Sir, um, remember you said that . . . thing . . . about the translation? The signature?" I said.

He smacked his lips, made a fist, and softly hit his desk. As if he had been on *our* side all along.

"Oh, yes, ugh, let me see."

"If it's okay with you, Sir, since it's not the end of the day. . . . We can go get it signed or get a new translation done and bring it back before the end of the day. Do you think . . . ? Would that be okay?" I tried to say it as nonchalantly as possible. Whatever he'd write in his report, I knew it would say that we had a real relationship, but we still needed the translator's signature. I took a chance while David held his breath next to me.

"You're a translator, right?"

"Yes, sir. I didn't translate it because I thought it would be a conflict of interest."

"I translated my wife's paperwork when I sent it in. No conflict."

As he said this, he took a blank paper from his printer and handed me a pen.

"Go ahead. Translate it."

I started translating and paced myself so I was not too quick or too sluggish. And David, who hardly ever initiates conversation, asked the officer about his life. I eavesdropped as I wrote. His wife was from Poland. They had two kids, and he mentioned our rent was more expensive than his mortgage. They discussed the rising prices in Connecticut and how the price goes down when you continue getting farther away from New York City. The officer's wife called him and he took out an old flip phone. Then I understood why he didn't understand you could text money. He had a short conversation with her and then, for some reason, began to talk to David about lawyering up.

"Nah, you didn't need a lawyer. Glad you mentioned the photos, though."

I signed my name on the translation of the birth certificate and announced I was done.

"Now it's complete. And you're both all set." He got up and ushered us into the main hallway.

When he was out of sight, I spread my arms out and hugged the wall. David leaned his back into it and undid the top button of shirt, exhaling as if he had just finished a sprint. We didn't say a word until we reached the car.

A week later, I opened the door to our apartment and found David sitting on a chair in our small dining room, still in his car wash uniform.

"It's here," he said.

"What? Already?" I said, while I dropped everything by the front door and ran to our kitchen table. Most couples had told us the green card arrived three weeks or even a month after the interview. Maybe it was the result I'd been dreading, but I kept quiet and told David it was time to open the envelope.

There was a letter congratulating David, an actual green card with the words PERMANENT RESIDENT on the top, and a pamphlet explaining the benefits associated with becoming a resident. We took turns looking at his head shot, making sure his name and birthday were correct, while I squealed. He continued to sit, but hugged me tight and placed his head on my stomach as I wove my hands through his hair. He looked up, fighting tears, and said: "Thank you."

"For what?" I said.

I relished my happiness, but the sour tinge of guilt soon rose in my throat. How many undocumented immigrants would never get to feel the relief of that hug? How many sons and daughters would continue to live with the fear that their parents might be gone tomorrow? We would love and live in our home, while others could be removed at any moment. David didn't deserve this anymore than other undocumented individuals. I knew it wasn't about *being deserving*, because our happiness stood on the foundations of privilege and luck. There would still be years, thousands of dollars in fees, and even more paperwork before David could apply for citizenship. The green card meant one day he could apply and, hopefully, obtain a paper that would say what he and many others around the country already knew about themselves: that they are, indeed, Americans.

WHEN I WAKE
FROM A DREAM WITH HIM

one of the first things I do is tell my husband. Failure to share the details weighs on me. Or maybe I just share so if he dreams of a former lover one day, he can feel free to describe it to me. He listens and laughs—his eyebrows rise up and down as if questioning my subconscious. I separate this imaginary world from reality by refusing to write about it on the notes app like I do with other dreams.

When I wake from a dream with him, words someone once said come to mind: *Waking life is considered a dream for our sleep selves.* Maybe, but then again, I never know when I'm dreaming. When I sleep, my dream-self picks up another life, one where he and I scream at each other, or I trip while he's chasing me, or we rewatch snippets of a trilogy we vowed to see together even if we'd broken up. Which we did, in real life, with his new girlfriend a few rows in front of us, and which we repeat in my dreams.

He's wearing a tight monochrome blue shirt, biceps bulging, brown skin tanned from the sun. But then I wake, in a different realm, with my husband next to me and a pounding headache. I've turned around so much the sheets have constricted themselves into restraints, keeping me tied to the bed. I don't know the difference between a déjà vu and a dream.

When I wake from a dream with him, I count how many years it's been since we saw each other. First it was two, then five, then seven, and now the amount of time I haven't seen him has much surpassed the almost year I was with him. If I'm now thirty-one and he's close to that, does that mean he has a double chin? I wake—wonder if he's a father. On days I don't dream about him, he doesn't enter my waking thoughts, but on the days I do, my conscious self gets upset with my sub-self for allowing him to be the first thing I think about. I learn how a dream can be a noun or a verb, but both are ephemeral.

When I wake from a dream with him I want to ask my friends whether they dream about their teenage loves too. Do their former lovers hunt them with an ax accompanied by staggering zombies? Do they appear with nothing but a towel, an abdominal *V* tight—beckoning—in an apartment where walls and doors are made of glass, the sun blaring through as if on a planet closer to the sun? I think about asking them, but afraid it'll spiral into tales of wet dreams, I keep them to myself.

When I wake from a dream with him and it's been three nights and, ugh, they've become too vivid, like the way the smell of gasoline triggers the possibility of danger—so sharp that I decide to mention them to my therapist, and then wonder how to phrase it: *Never the same dream twice, and rarely sensual, sexual, whatever, with a few exceptions, but it's—it's as if we're still together because we fight, and he's there like that damn squirrel in* Ice Age, *and maybe I'm the acorn, or maybe I'm the tree where the acorn comes from, or maybe this comparison doesn't make sense, but I'm just wondering, how do I pull him out of my brain if I don't think about him while I'm awake—just on the days he's there before I open my eyes—you know, because, listen, I just really need this to stop.*

When I wake from a dream with him, I wonder why I don't dream of my spouse more. Why his present flesh is not explored by my intuition. Maybe because I know he'll be here tomorrow, slipping his hand to my left breast under my Galapagos pajama as we sleep.

When I wake from a dream with him, I suspect many therapy sessions will be needed to end this. My therapist asks me if I, deep down, need to say something to him. *No, truly.* She answers: *Then you don't dream of him, you just put your problems on his face.* I expect months of unthreading, of peeling back the layers like a red onion and then deciding whether to cut in brunoise or mince, but no matter what, tears will sprout. This doesn't happen. *Did anything traumatizing occur while you were with him?* she says. *Ha!* I say. *A lot.* I list the losses—just so much loss—the way I cried myself to sleep every night and how he was the only one there for me. Then he left too. I share how I clung to my need of him. *Maybe you didn't love him. He was just grounding you, and then you felt abandoned within a time of continuous trauma.* I didn't think we could squeeze the onion to sticky liquid in the first session, but we make the pulp bloom.

When I wake from a dream with him and then speak to a professional, I realize the dreams are just the vestiges of it all.

When I wake from a dream with him for too long, it doesn't dawn on me they could stop. A week after the therapy session, I think it's too good to be true that he doesn't appear, still prepared for his deep voice, the memory of his rough cologne. But they never come. Instead, snakes weave into compartments of a house I've never been in but I know is mine. Another night, my father doesn't believe a confession I can't say in waking life. The ground crumbles underneath me and I land in the wet of a helter-skelter after a light rain. My husband cleans the pool before kissing my dimples, then we tele-transport to Ecuador and learn how to love each other within the dense heat.

(UN)DOCUMENTED

After Adriana Páramo

Animals

> *These are not people. These are animals.*
> —The 45th president of the United States

The administration tries to clarify that those words refer to only *some* migrants, but I know he means all of us. And so I wait for fangs to replace my teeth, look over to my husband as we wake and wonder if that will be the day I see a huddle of spider eyes have sprouted on his forehead. I wait for my dad to tell me he has grown a tail. For my husband's uncle to say fish skin has flourished in the spaces between his fingers, and that the ocean beckons him, his hands now fins. For friends who have crossed the border to tell me that their toes are morphing into the tough of hooves.

I wait and wait and wait, not realizing that for many we've been animals even before we were born.

BoPET

BoPET (biaxially-oriented polyethylene terephthalate) is the material of the emergency blanket that was developed for NASA and is commonly known as Mylar. Uses on Earth: Stabilize runners' temperature after a marathon, melt snow, create a shelter, insert into gloves and boots while hiking to insulate from the cold, use as a signaling device when lost in the woods, reflect heat, give to detained brown children at the border for them to stay warm while they wonder if they'll see their mothers again. It may only weigh 1.75 ounces, but have you ever felt the heaviness of a blanket that isn't yours?

Citizenship

*Abridged List of Alternative Questions
for the US Naturalization Test*

How many times does the word *alien* appear in federal documents and laws?

How much does it cost to build a wall/fence/invisible demarcation along the US-Mexico border?

How long has ICE been in existence?

Say another word that begins with the word *alien* that is not *alienate*.

List antonyms to *life*, *liberty*, and *the pursuit of happiness*.

Describe the 100-Mile Border Zone.

What is the definition of "Freedom of Movement" according to the Universal Declaration of Human Rights?

How many children have been separated from their guardians at the border?

Approximately how many undocumented individuals reside in the United States?

Who is Gilberto Francisco Ramos Juárez?

DREAMer

Fill out paperwork. Send $495 to the US government. Get your fingerprints done in another state because it's the closest location. Wait until the police background check goes through. Get a card in the mail. It's not a green card but a work permit in red, white, and blue like the country's flag that has formed you but not birthed you. Avoid getting parking tickets, don't bump into any cops, and leave whenever a fight breaks out at a bar. Lawyer's orders, right? You don't want to be implicated. At work, don't use the word "undocumented." Pretend your childhood was just like Kathy's, who sits in the cubicle across from you and has lived in the same house her entire life. Accept that you can't think about five or ten years down the line because you need to renew your DACA application every two years. And, let's face it, maybe DACA will be rescinded. Then there won't even be a cubicle with your name on it anymore. Sometimes you question whether a path that ends is better than no path at all.

Esperar

"To wait."

While David waits for paperwork to be processed throughout the years, he trudges on. Some moments he's painfully aware of the possibility of deportation looming over him; throughout others, the uncertainty fades into the background. He meets with friends from Costa Rica on a rooftop in New York City to talk about moments from long ago that involve scraped knees and soccer matches on hot pavement. We visit museums where there are off-kilter sculptures of debris within luggage and where we can eat the art. We have a cupcake fight with David's guardians, ending his birthday with smears of cake on our cheeks and icing trickling into the crevices of our ears while our chuckles persist. He spends the weekend drifting around a track, the flecks of tires burned off and embedded into his forehead. In the moments that he waits, there is love and laughter and hope.

Freedom University

By federal law, all K–12 public schools must open their doors to undocumented youth. States around the country have their own laws regarding public colleges and universities. Texas, Washington, Hawaii, California, Connecticut, and others have some form of tuition support for undocumented youth. Some states allow undocumented students to attend as foreign students, which means no one applies due to extravagant tuition fees. Georgia, though, bans undocumented individuals from public colleges and universities altogether.

In 2011, Freedom University was created by undocumented youth and allies to provide college classes to undocumented youth in Georgia. One of their classes is "Human Rights and Immigration in the United States," a topic the students live first and study later. Spring 2019 courses: Neuroscience, Spanish Literature, Calculus, Human Rights and Legal Studies, Freedom University Mural Project, Son Jarocho Music Ensemble: Son de sueños. Freedom University held a campaign that led Emory University to become the first private university to allow DACA recipients to attend college with access to financial aid.

They continue to tell Georgia they're here to stay.

Green Card

My future husband arrives in the United States as a teen in 2006.

He receives Deferred Action for Childhood Arrivals (DACA) status in 2012.

He renews it two years later.

We marry in 2016, and I file a petition on his behalf for permanent residency.

He becomes a conditional permanent resident in 2017 and is granted a two-year green card.

In February 2019 he applies to remove the conditions on his status.

On February 18, 2020, he receives a letter granting permanent residency.

Fourteen years to receive a ten-year green card.

Maybe he'll become a citizen by the fifteenth.

Home

A house is a home, except for children who wonder whether Mom and Dad will still be there when they get off the school bus. When people ask where they are from, they hesitate.

Is it their mother's womb?

The land they first walked on?

Or the land they live on?

Imperil

On Valentine's Day, during a chilly night where the sky lacks clouds, we hear a blast from David's car and he screeches to the emergency lane. We've been dating for more than a year, and this is the first time our concerns regarding safety diverge. I ask him how we'll get to his home. He asks me to pretend to be the driver—to switch seats—in case the cops come. I want to say: *But you already have a driver's license and haven't been drinking.* But his panic makes me acquiesce. Just the tow truck appears, and the man leads us off the highway then leaves the damaged car outside David's house as our adrenaline starts to taper off. In the warmth of his bed, he mentions that any wrong move can imperil his life. Even if it's just one accident. Even if no other car is involved. I nod and tell him I can never understand how he feels. But that I'll be there.

Joy

David's guardians leave Connecticut after living here for more than fifteen years. They've rented since the moment they arrived, and they will continue to rent, but in a hotter state where the windchill doesn't hover around the teens in the winter. I don't ask why they don't return to Costa Rica because I already know the answer. They want to be able to embrace David in a hug every few months when we visit them down south. Their first grandchild has just been born, and they want to see if his curls will remain tight or if they'll loosen up as the months pass. They want to see whether or not he'll have dimples. They want to be present for his first steps. They stay because the joy outweighs the uncertainty.

Kin

Absence is difficult to describe because it encapsulates what is not there. What never happened. This is what I think about when next of kin—children and parents— meet in the corridors of airports after months, some- times a year, of being separated at the border. It makes me uncomfortable to watch the photos and videos, but I still look at them. I visualize moments that never came to pass. No outings to eat rum raisin ice cream that runs down a cake cone until the melt makes a trail along a kid's wrist. No hugs before going to sleep. No learning how to multiply with Dad's help. No mother pushing a swing as a harsh rain begins, then holding hands and running to the car. I think about families who will never see each other again. Moments that only exist in a realm of what-ifs. All that has been stolen from them.

License

As of 2021, sixteen states and the District of Columbia allow undocumented immigrants to obtain a license to drive. Ricardo's wife, Melanie, asks my mother to do him a favor. Can he use her address in Connecticut as his home address, even though he's working in North Carolina? In a few months he'll come to take a driver's test. Every few weeks my mother sends him the stack of mail she receives under his name. A few months later, he stops by and apologizes for being a nuisance. He leaves with a Connecticut license, ease settling into his bones, but not for too long. He'll need to renew it in a few years, and if he's ever stopped in his state, he'll pretend he's just a visitor. Always a visitor.

Migrants

The parents of at least 2,654 migrant children under the Zero-Tolerance Policy are left to wonder why they could no longer see their kids or hug them or play with them or laugh with them. The youngest child is barely four months old. Our nation separates infants from their mothers and fathers before they can pronounce their names. Children are taken from their parents and placed into cages. Parents are deported without their sons and daughters. Children are separated from their families as a deterrent, and time is used to sever ties that may never mend. Beginning in April 2018 at the US-Mexico border, babies are separated from their mothers before they can memorize their scent.

Niños

Jakelin Caal Maquin. Died on December 8, 2018, in US custody. Seven years old. Born in the Guatemalan town of Raxruhá of the Q'eqchi' Indigenous people.

Darlyn Cristabel Cordova-Valle. Died on September 29, 2018, in US custody. Ten years old. Born in El Salvador.

Felipe Gómez Alonzo. Died on December 24, 2018, in US custody. Eight years old. Born in the Guatemalan province of Huehuetenango of the Chuj Indigenous people.

Carlos Hernández Vásquez. Died on May 20, 2019, in US custody. Sixteen years old. Born in the Guatemalan town of San José El Rodeo.

Juan de León Gutiérrez. Died on April 30, 2019, in US custody. Sixteen years old. Born in the Guatemalan municipality of Camotán of the Ch'orti' Indigenous people.

Wilmer Josué Ramírez Vásquez. Died on May 14, 2019, a few weeks after being released from US custody. Two years old. Born in the Guatemalan municipality of Olopa.

Over

Years after a paper arrives saying that he's a permanent resident, I ask David how it feels. If it's like a part of his life was over and done with once he received it. *There are two sides to it,* he says. *Yes, there's a part that allows me to live without being afraid, and I'm grateful for that. But I still think about that time. The fear. I try to remind myself of where I come from. It's not something anyone should forget.*

Prayer

I listen to the podcast *Room 20.* When I start it, I only know that it's about identifying a man who has been in a vegetative state in California since 1999. For almost seventeen years, no one knew his name or where he was born. An investigative reporter, Joanne Faryon, makes it a goal to find out as much as she can about the man nick-named, as if he were a thing and not a human, 66 Garage.

After months of research, she finds out his name is Ignacio. He's an undocumented migrant who was riding in the back of a truck in California that collided with another vehicle when the driver tried to speed away from the Border Patrol. One man lost his life and three more were injured, including Ignacio. For years, no next of kin visited him. No one called him by his name. For years he only felt the touch of the doctors and nurses who reposi-tioned him around his bed. It wasn't until 2016, through the help of Faryon and the Border Angels organization, that a next of kin was found. His sister, Juliana, was sure Ignacio had died trying to cross the border. She also crossed the border many decades ago and lives in Ohio as an undocumented immigrant. Like many others, she refrained from contacting police or government officials to find out about her brother, afraid that it would jeopar-dize her life and result in her own deportation.

When I finish listening, I say a prayer to those who tried to cross the border never to be heard from again. I say a prayer because sometimes I feel like that's all I can do.

Q'anjob'al

They come with tongues that don't speak Spanish or English. Languages like Q'anjob'al, Mam, K'iche', all of which are spoken predominantly in Guatemala. In court, migrants stand before judges, lawyers, and strangers deciphering what they're saying through their eyes, the lines across their foreheads, and mouths that refuse to smile. Decisions are made about their lives without their comprehension. If they're fortunate, relay interpreting is available. An individual interprets from English to Spanish and another individual interprets from Spanish to the migrant's language. This is costly and unusual—but necessary. Many lawyers can't even communicate with their clients. Many of the migrants sign papers with words that look like hieroglyphics. Later, when officers refuse to let them see their children, they realize they have relinquished their parental rights.

Remembrance

When going to a funeral is out of the question, all that's left is remembrance. When my husband's cousin dies before he has a green card, all he can do is mourn him through photos and by playing his favorite song. All I do is hold David's hands and wipe tears from his cheeks. There's nothing I can say. There's nothing I can do to make it better. And as he takes deep breaths between sobs, I wonder how many eulogies have been uttered thousands of miles away from a funeral. I wonder how many memories can never be created with loved ones who are still breathing, all because of man-made borders.

Sapito

Ricardo doesn't know how to thank my mother after years of mail with his name on it gets sent to her home. My mother says that it's nothing, that this is what friends do, but one day he comes bearing a gift. It's a large wooden box that almost looks like a seat for a kid, except it's not meant for sitting. It has a long lid with a sapo sculpture on it, a frog painted in a bronze-like color with its mouth hanging open. The number "1,000" appears next to the sapo, and it's surrounded by circles, each with their own number—lowest toward the front, highest to the back. The task is to throw metal rings into each of the holes from feet away, and the sapito's mouth is the jackpot. I know that Ricardo is a carpenter and lives in a house he built himself, and although I've never met him, I picture a man taking the time to saw wood, painting the box an opaque green, and making sure the white-painted numbers are legible. Even though it's not meant for me, I ask my mother to thank Ricardo, and to please invite him over for a barbecue and to play a game of sapito. I'd love to meet him.

Taxes

Before my husband gets his papers, he pays taxes for years. Taxes that go to support the local government, the state, the nation. Undocumented immigrants don't have a Social Security number, but they file their taxes with Individual Taxpayer Identification Numbers (ITINs). In 2015, $13.6 billion in taxes were filed by individuals with ITINs. Nevertheless, David is ineligible for health insurance or tuition assistance. One day, when he laughs so hard his mouth opens wide, I see it. One of his molars hangs by a small corner, as if a tiny sword hasn't finished its job. It doesn't hurt him, he assures me, and he won't go to the dentist until pain sets in. He has no insurance. He has no credit card. I beg him to borrow mine. I say, *Please, you can pay me back whenever. Just go.*

The molar can't be saved and the removal costs eight hundred dollars, less than what he pays in taxes that same year.

Unmarked

The Sacred Heart Cemetery in Falfurrias, Texas, holds bodies of unidentified undocumented migrants. While some migrants successfully cross the border into the United States, many of them don't survive the heat in the last stretch to evade the Border Patrol. Stiff bodies are picked up by sun-soaked shrubs around Brooks County, and bodies are placed in unmarked graves. Some of the deceased end up placed in a coffin or a funeral bag. Some are laid to rest in all types of garbage bags. In 2013 forensic scientists from two universities arrive to exhume bodies. They find fifty bodies in ten days, and only afterward does the process of identification begin.

Visible

Undocumented people are graphic designers, chefs, poets, storytellers, personal trainers, lawyers, advocates, singers, doctors. You speak to them every day. A teacher may have an undocumented student worried about whether her parents will be deported. A new coworker may come from a mixed-status family where he is the only one of his siblings that doesn't have a Social Security number. The driver who took you to the airport last month may only have a side job so he can pay the lawyer's fee to fix his papers. Undocumented individuals are everywhere. They are not living in the shadows—many people just refuse to believe they work, live, and breathe alongside them.

Wall

Starting in April 2013 until November 2017, a maintenance door is opened six times at Friendship Park, where the border wall divides Tijuana, Mexico, and San Diego, California. The wall is more like a fence within a fence. Slabs of concrete point up toward the sky and are accompanied by double-welded wire mesh between the spaces, not large enough for fingers to pass through. Most of the time, when the maintenance door is closed, husbands and wives have dates where they can hear and see each other but never touch. The wires of the wall blur their faces so much it's as if they aren't even in the same place. But for some minutes, each of the six times they open the maintenance door dubbed the Door of Hope, relatives who might not have seen each other for years are able to feel the warmth of their loved ones.

The first time the door is opened, Luis Angulo hugs his five-year-old daughter, Jimena. In a photo, Jimena is seen on the Mexican side with black pants and a sweater blazoned in streaks of purple, staring at her father, a man she had only seen and heard but had never touched. In the last door-opening event, a man in the United States and a woman from Mexico get married and kiss, while border agents clad in green are present with stoic faces. According to the *Los Angeles Times*, 2017 is the last time the Door of Hope is opened, with the chief of the San Diego Border Patrol asserting: "Moving forward, the maintenance gate will be used for maintenance purposes only."

Ximenez

I don't remember how I meet Susie Ximenez. Maybe online or through a friend of a friend. She's the program coordinator of the organization Adelante Student Voices based in New York and the founder of Latinx Project. She's undocumented, a graphic designer, a parent, an activist, and much more. We hike together, talk about our families and our goals. I'm astounded at everything she accomplishes for her local community. She foments a space where undocumented individuals can reach out to inquire about paths to citizenship and ways to attend college, while also showcasing their artwork. In 2018 she organizes a free event for the Day of the Dead where community members can contribute to an altar. The following year, she oversees the exhibition "Bajo la misma luna," which showcases art by undocumented youth. She lives by the words she writes: "We rise by lifting one another."

Years

My friend has been in the country for years. Almost two decades. When she tells me she's leaving, I don't say, *Please no, stay,* although I want to. It would be selfish of me to ask that of her. Instead I say, *I'll miss you,* and, *I'm glad you decided to do what feels right.* Friends and family members have left of their own volition, knowing that it would be years, most likely a decade, until they can come back to the United States. As time passed, she tried to continue her life within the limitations of what it meant to be undocumented. But with DACA, and how administrations continue to bounce back between eliminating the program and paving a way to citizenship, she says she can't bear the limbo anymore. Months before her departure, she tells me how much she looks forward to a life without the fear that a program will make or break her chances of continuing to reside and work where she has chosen. This is the path of liberation she has forged, one some decide to take instead of waiting for a resolution that at times feels like it will never come to pass.

Z_____

A word that starts with the letter *Z* would imply there is an end. But I can't will myself to choose if the end isn't real. As I write these words, the Dream and Promise Act has just passed the House, but ambivalence lingers within the undocumented community, especially since the first law of this type was introduced in 2001—two decades ago. The end isn't real because there are people being deported at the border as I edit this essay. The end isn't real because if the Dream Act passes, it won't include all undocumented people living in the United States. The end isn't real because ICE still exists. The end isn't real because allowing children to become citizens, but not their parents, only results in fractured families. The end isn't real because not all the children who were separated from their parents during the enforcement of the Zero-Tolerance Policy have been reunited with their loved ones. There is no ending. This essay doesn't end. The end will arrive when the eleven million undocumented people can feel safe in their homes.

EPILOGUE:
A LETTER FOR MY FATHER

Dear Papi,

Do you remember when I stopped calling you Papi? I've always wondered if you noticed. I could never call you Father or Padre or Pops or Daddy. Sometimes I say Dad, but only when you make a joke I don't like and have no other choice but to yell *Daaaaad*. Do you remember when I could hardly talk to you some years ago? I just responded with syllables. Sí. No. No sé. Okay. Está bien. I was so mad at you. For so many reasons. But the anger has dwindled, and now I talk to a therapist about it instead of a shaman. Now we're both here in the United States. Can you believe it? You always say that you never know what's going to happen today or tomorrow or next year. That we have to enjoy life to the fullest no matter what comes our way. To let go of the bile and anger. You always tell me not to dwell. But I'm a writer, and that's what we do; we dwell.

Papi, I'm writing you this letter because there are just some things I can't sit down with you and say. Just like when you used to play songs in your car that weren't actually songs. They were stories, sometimes fables, about life. Sometimes they were poems with violins or accordions streaming in the background. I remember hearing the words *Caminante, son tus huellas el camino y nada más* in your truck. You were the one that told me that before that became a famous song called "Cantares" by Joan Manuel Serrat, it was a poem. A poem by the great Antonio Machado.

After you played this poem song, you made me listen to a story about a family. It was about a mom and dad and a few kids. The narrator began to describe their home, but more importantly, the moment the family would sit down and eat. There were two tables. One for the mom and dad and all the kids. And another one for the grandma or grandpa, who was frail and made a mess when they ate. It was so no one would feel disgust when the elder spilled water and food from their mouth. And this is how they ate every day. I remember we had parked outside our house and the track hadn't finished, my hand ready to open the door, and gently, in a calm voice, you told me not to leave the car until I listened to the whole thing. It turns out that the father sees one of his children playing around with some wood from their yard. The kid isn't really doing anything, just placing them in blocks to make it look like a bench or desk. The father interrupts the kid and asks what he's doing. The boy responds: "Building a table for when you get old." By the time the song ended, we were both sobbing because I knew you couldn't sit down with me to enunciate how you felt. But this was your way of showing me why. The why behind everything. And I want you to know that I understand, Papi. I would have done the same for Abuelo too. I'll always be here for you, just like how you were there for him.

I want to tell you about another memory I have that I've never shared with anyone. Not Mom, or my best friends, or David. I've kept it with me for many years, but I want you to know. We were still living in the condominiums by the train station in South Norwalk. I opened my eyes in the middle of the night to see Alonso a few feet away from me. Do you remember him? He was one of the many strangers that ceased to be strangers when they came to live with us. You and my mom always helped people whenever you could. Well, he was a few feet away and it seemed like he was trying to wake me up with a whisper. As if he was too afraid to get close. I get it. He was an older man, with glasses that constantly slipped from his nose and curly hair, and I was probably nine or ten. He kept his distance and kept repeating my name. But sleep kept me on the bed until I heard him say, "There's a fire. We have to leave. Now. Vamos, Vicky." I followed him out of the apartment and went to the entrance as I held his hand and looked for you, my brother, and my mom.

Everyone stood by all the parked cars of the huge parking lot, which seemed more like a motel parking lot than that of a garage. Then I saw Mom and held her leg as tight as I could as we watched and she held my brother in her arms. I couldn't see a fire, but fingers pointed to the second floor, and we all looked up at the smoke floating from an apartment's open windows. People stood and watched in blue pajamas and flip-flops as firefighters trudged in. Just like those before me, I stood in awe, the despair of starting over already seeping into my stomach. I thought about my toys, my bed, and the room the four of us shared. I couldn't think of tomorrow or even an hour from then. I was paralyzed in the loss of the moment.

You appeared in your lime green truck and I heard people laughing. "Damn, he's ready, huh?" someone said. I didn't understand until I looked back. You were the only one not standing or fidgeting but driving, moving. *Caminante, no hay camino, se hace camino al andar.* You told us to get in the car. And although Alonso stayed, Mom and I ran toward you. I went into the tight backseat as I stared through the windows. You were about ready to hit the gas when someone told you to stop. I could see the back of your head while you faced the street beyond the condo road, as if there was nothing important to look back to. Alonso got closer and said maybe the fire wouldn't burn the buildings down. And suddenly a woman strode out from her apartment coughing as someone, maybe a firefighter, maybe an EMT—I can't quite recall—grabbed her in the outdoor hallway before she could fall. I think she was taken to the hospital, but people eased their way back into their apartments, the adrenaline fueling a night of insomnia.

This is what I envision when I think about the essence of you. Not lingering in the past. Not thinking about the what-ifs. *Al andar se hace camino*. Just doing. I've always envied you for that. Do you know that sometimes David calls me Reinalda? He says I am very much like you. Quick to get riled up just like a fosforito. Funny. Intense. But I think that I lack the qualities that I most adore about you. Continuing. Jumping up to the opportunity. Being so confident and sure in everything that you do. Marching ahead while the people around you are telling you to look back. I'm still trying, now that I'm more than thirty, to be more like you. Not in all ways, of course. But I look up to you. I hope that when life hands me a fire that I'll know not to rise from the ashes. But, like you, to wait for the wind to saunter away the remains of what was once sturdy and not even dare to look back at it. *Y al volver la vista atrás se ve la senda que nunca se ha de volver de pisar.* And then, with new wood, whether from maple or guayacán, we'll craft a new foundation. I mean, we're Ecuadorians, after all. Right, Papi? We burn the past at least once in our lives.

Tu hija,
Victoria

ACKNOWLEDGMENTS

The utmost gratitude to Shara McCallum for choosing this book as the winner of the Fairfield Book Prize and to the entire team at Woodhall Press for publishing this memoir in essays.

This book would not exist without the guidance of the Fairfield University MFA program. A special thank-you to Carol Ann Davis, Sonya Huber, Eugenia Kim, Dinty W. Moore, Susan Muaddi Darraj, Adriana Páramo, Lynn Steger Strong, and all my workshop peers for their heartfelt and generous feedback while I wrote this book. I'm beyond grateful for the community I have found on Enders Island.

Para mis familiares y amigos en Ecuador, les agradezco por su constante apoyo. A mi madrina, Victoria Buitrón, gracias por contestar mis mil preguntas sobre nuestra familia y por las anécdotas compartidas. A mis tíos y primos, los Casal y Santamaría, por todo el amor que me han demostrado con el paso de los años. A mis queridos amigos de la universidad—especialmente a María Fernanda Freire, Angelike Páez y Johnny Troya—

por creer en mí cuando ni se me ocurría escribir un libro. A todos mis queridos amigos milagreños, especialmente a la familia Serrano-Reinel, por abrir las puertas de su casa y tratarme como una hija más.

Thank you, most of all, to my immediate family, Mom, Dad, and Bro, for your unwavering support.

David, sometimes I wonder if one life with you will be enough. I thank the universe I found you.

Abuelo, this book is for you. Everything is for you. Un día nos volveremos a ver.

SOURCES

Blitzer, Jonathan, et al. "An Underground College for Undocumented Immigrants." *The New Yorker*. www.newyorker.com/magazine/2017/05/22/an-underground-college-for-undocumented-immigrants.

Bort, Ryan. "These Family Reunification Videos Show the Horror of Trump's Border Policy." *Rolling Stone*, 17 July 2018. www.rollingstone.com/politics/politics-news/family-reunification-videos-699565/.

Brigida, Anna-Catherine. "A Guatemalan Teen Fled Climate Change. He Died in U.S. Custody." *Time*, 13 May 2019. www.time.com/5587817/juan-de-leon-gutierrez-guatemala-migrant/.

Carcamo, Cindy. "Ancient Mayan Languages Are Creating Problems for Today's Immigration Courts." *Los Angeles Times*, 9 August 2016. www.latimes.com/local/california/la-me-mayan-indigenous-languages-20160725-snap-story.html.

"Chapter 3—United States Citizens at Birth (INA 301 and 309)." *USCIS*, 5 March 2020. www.uscis.gov/policy-manual/volume-12-part-h-chapter-3.

"Courses." Freedom University. freedom-university.org/courses.

@cristinariofri3. "In america, i can speak FUCKING spanish if i want to." Twitter, 21 September 2019, 10:09 p.m.. twitter.com/cristinariofri3/status/1175592917022457856. Accessed 25 March 2020.

Dickerson, Caitlin. "The Youngest Child Separated from His Family at the Border Was 4 Months Old." *New York Times*, 16 June 2019. www.nytimes.com/2019/06/16/us/baby-constantine-romania-migrants.html. Accessed 16 June 2019.

"Episode 3: The Border." *Room 20* from Los Angeles Times Studio, 1 August 2019. www.wondery.com/shows/room-20/.

"Episode 5: The Reunion." *Room 20* from Los Angeles Times Studio, 13 August 2019. www.wondery.com/shows/room-20/.

"Family Separation by the Numbers." *American Civil Liberties Union*, 2 October 2018. www.aclu.org/issues/immigrants-rights/immigrants-rights-and-detention/family-separation.

Flores, Adolfo. "Separated Parents Were 'Totally Unaware' They Had Waived Their Right to Be Reunified with Their Children." *BuzzFeed News*, 3 August 2018. www.buzzfeednews.com/article/adolfoflores/separated-parents-totally-unaware-they-had-waived-their.

Frey, John Carlos. "Graves of Shame." *Texas Observer*, 6 July 2015. www.texasobserver.org/illegal-mass-graves-of-migrant-remains-found-in-south-texas/.

Hennessy-Fiske, Molly. "Six Migrant Children Have Died in U.S. Custody. Here's What We Know About Them." *Los Angeles Times*, 24 May 2019. www.latimes.com/nation/la-na-migrant-child-border-deaths-20190524-story.html.

Ignatow, Gabe, and Alexander T. Williams. "New Media and the 'Anchor Baby' Boom." *Journal of Computer-Mediated Communication*, vol. 17, no. 1, October 2011: 60–76. doi.org/10.1111/j.1083-6101.2011.01557.x.

Korte, Gregory, and Alan Gomez. "Trump Ramps up Rhetoric on Undocumented Immigrants: 'These Aren't People. These Are Animals.'" *USA Today*, Gannett Satellite Information Network, 17 May 2018. www.usatoday.com/story/news/politics/2018/05/16/trump-immigrants-animals-mexico-democrats-sanctuary-cities/617252002/.

Malkin, Elisabeth. "In Home Village of Girl Who Died in U.S. Custody, Poverty Drives Migration." *New York Times*, 19 December 2018. www.nytimes.com/2018/12/18/world/americas/migrant-jakelin-guatemala-border.html.

"Man Fired After Racist Remarks Go Viral." WPTV, 27 September 2019. www.wptv.com/news/local-news/watercooler/man-fired-after-racist-remarks-go-viral.

Mendoza, Gilbert, and Chesterfield Polkey. "States Offering Driver's Licenses to Immigrants." National Conference of State Legislatures, 25 July 2019. www.ncsl.org/research/immigration/states-offering-driver-s-licenses-to-immigrants.aspx.

Moore, Robert, and Maria Sacchetti. "Toddler Who Died after Being Taken into Custody at the Mexican Border Suffered Multiple Diseases." *Washington Post*, 2 July 2019. www.washingtonpost.com/immigration/toddler-who-died-after-being-taken-into-custody-at-the-mexican-border-suffered-multiple-diseases/2019/07/02/5fda6674-9d03-11e9-9ed4-c9089972ad5a_story.html.

Moran, Greg. "Border Gate Opened for First Time in Years." Chicagotribune.com. *Chicago Tribune*, 28 April 2013. www.chicagotribune.com/sdut-border-gate-opened-for-first-time-in-years-2013apr28-story.html.

Morrissey, Kate. "'Door of Hope' Is Closed to Cross-Border Hugs and Weddings." *Los Angeles Times*, 6 January 2018. www.latimes.com/local/lanow/la-me-ln-sd-door-of-hope-20180106-story.html.

Páramo, Adriana. *Looking for Esperanza: the Story of a Mother, a Child Lost, and Why They Matter to Us*. Benu Press, 2012.

Pear, Robert. "President Signs Landmark Bill on Immigration." *New York Times*, 7 November 1986. www.nytimes.com/1986/11/07/us/president-signs-landmark-bill-on-immigration.html.

Perez, Sonia. "Father of Dead Guatemalan Boy Heard Rumors They Could Cross." *AP NEWS*, Associated Press, 28 December 2018. apnews.com/7b429e3d3509460a8e2dd241de0c5120.

@realDonaldTrump. "An 'extremely credible source' has called my office and told me that @BarackObama's birth certificate is a fraud." Twitter, 6 August 2012, 4:23 p.m. twitter.com/realDonaldTrump/status/232572505238433794.

Rose, Joel. "Trump Administration Travel Ban Expands to 6 Additional Countries." *NPR*, 31 January 2020. www.npr.org/2020/01/31/801687700/trump-administration-travel-ban-expands-to-6-additional-countries.

Soltis, Laura Emiko. "Freedom University: Educating Undocumented Young People in Georgia." *Forbes*, 16 November 2017. www.forbes.com/sites/ashoka/2017/11/16/freedom-university-educating-undocumented-young-people-in-georgia/#78d98b964c20.

Soria Mendoza, Gilberto, and Noor Shaikh. "Tuition Benefits for Immigrants." National Conference of State Legislature, 1 March 2021. www.ncsl.org/research/immigration/tuition-benefits-for-immigrants.aspx.

Tran, Mai. "Guilty Plea Highlights Scams to Get Visas through Marriage." *Los Angeles Times*, 7 August 2006. www.latimes.com/archives/la-xpm-2006-aug-07-me-brides7-story.html.

"Trump Immigration Executive Order: President Wants to Terminate Birthright Citizenship." YouTube. Uploaded by Axios, 30 October 2018. www.youtube.com/watch?v=H0d21nQBY8o.

"Undocumented Immigrants Are Paying Their Taxes Today, Too." CNN, 19 April 2019. www.cnn.com/2019/04/15/us/taxes-undocumented-immigrants/index.html.

United States District Court, District of New Hampshire. *Hollander v. McCain et al.* CV-08-99-JL. 2008. www.washingtonpost.com/wp-srv/politics/documents/mccain_hollander_041708.pdf.

"What Does Anchor Baby Mean?" Dictionary.com, 23 December 2019. www.dictionary.com/e/slang/anchor-baby/.